8/26/12

MW00949411

To Eunice

My dear,

I have truly enjoyed our
journey + loved our fellowship.
I look forward to seeing
all the beauty that shall be
revealed throughout. You are an
"awesome" sister + friend...

Continue to be faithful
and see the fruits + enjoy
the fruits of your labor...

Much love
Always

Being Found in Him!

RENE' GLORIA HOOD

WestBow
PRESS
A DIVISION OF THOMAS NELSON

Copyright © 2012 by Rene' Gloria Hood.

All rights reserved. No part of this book may be used or reproduced by any means, graphic, electronic, or mechanical, including photocopying, recording, taping or by any information storage retrieval system without the written permission of the publisher except in the case of brief quotations embodied in critical articles and reviews.

Edited by: DerShaun Blanding

Foreword by: Peggy Joyce Ruth
Author of: Psalms 91, Those Who Trust the Lord Shall Not Be Disappointed and other wonderful books

Cover Photo by: Brenda D. Green

WestBow Press books may be ordered through booksellers or by contacting:

WestBow Press
A Division of Thomas Nelson
1663 Liberty Drive
Bloomington, IN 47403
www.westbowpress.com
1-(866) 928-1240

Because of the dynamic nature of the Internet, any web addresses or links contained in this book may have changed since publication and may no longer be valid. The views expressed in this work are solely those of the author and do not necessarily reflect the views of the publisher, and the publisher hereby disclaims any responsibility for them.

Any people depicted in stock imagery provided by Thinkstock are models, and such images are being used for illustrative purposes only.

Certain stock imagery © Thinkstock.

ISBN: 978-1-4497-5514-0 (hc)
ISBN: 978-1-4497-5513-3 (sc)
ISBN: 978-1-4497-5512-6 (e)

Library of Congress Control Number: 2012910119

Printed in the United States of America

WestBow Press rev. date: 06/25/2012

Table of Contents

Dedication

I would first like to dedicate this book for the lifting up of Jesus and the Glorifying of the Father. Without redemption I would not be able to have these testimonies, nor this song.

I would like to dedicate this book to my "mommy" who showed me her love through her spirit of servitude. She was truly the Proverbs 31 mother. She would wake before the dawn to prepare for her family. She would leave for work knowing that her babies were clean and full.

She was not perfect, but her love was. Her love embraced me and helped shape me into the woman that I am today. Her many acts of kindness, long-suffering, and forbearance give me a temperament sent from above. She gave me roots that will never be removed. Even though she has gone to heaven, she lives each and every day in my being. She first carried me inside of her and nourished me. Now, I carry her inside of me. The nourishment deposited in me by her has been made manifest by the Grace of God.

I also dedicate this book to my dad who is 78 years old as I write. He taught me the value of quality time. My dad spent time with his children. He wanted girls; and God gave him four girls and a boy. He showed me that a family spends time together. That they invest in each other and they are there for each other. When I got saved I knew that my heavenly Father had to really be extraordinary because my earthly dad would do whatever he could to make sure that I was alright. He has his faults, as we all do, but his deposit to me was a desire for a true relationship.

I also dedicate this book to my daughter; De'Nina Rene' who would not leave my side for fear that I was about to leave hers. Words could never express the thanksgiving I have toward God for allowing me to give birth to someone that is so rich in love, sincere in commitment, and full of desires toward Him and His purpose for her life. Nina, I will love you forever and thank you for my two wonderful granddaughters: Lyric & Chloe.

I would like to also dedicate this book to my son; Joshua Emmanuel who will find the time to text or call to say "I love you" and it feels as if all of his being came in agreement to make that proclamation. I know that God's seed is in you and I know that you will fulfill your destiny.

I want to personally give thanks and appreciation to my girlfriend Brenda Green who takes the word *friend* and manifests its meaning with so many acts of love. To Jennifer my friend and prayer partner, you have and should always be a special gift from God. Cindy you always let me know that you carry me in your heart and thoughts continually. Elise, we've journeyed from sin to salvation and our friendship was the better for it. I love all of you and you all were sent from God "just for me!"

I would also like to thank Apostle Dennis and Prophet Staci Houston for all of their love and fellowship through the years. My wonderful friend and fellow laborer in ROJ Ministry, Pastor Richard DuQue. There is no one like him and I appreciate all he does.

Last but not least, I would like to dedicate this book to all those who allowed the enemy to use them to try to destroy me and prevent me from walking in my destiny. God said it in Romans and He meant it—

All things work together for the good!

Epigraph

Philippians 3:9-10 *And **being found in him**, not having mine own righteousness which is the law, but that which is through the faith of Christ, the righteousness which is of God by faith. That I may know him, and the power of his resurrection, and the fellowship of his sufferings, being made conformable unto his death; If by any means I might attain unto the resurrection of the dead.*

Jesus defeated **"Lupus" and all diseases** at the cross! He gives us power to stand victoriously while dealing with abuse, betrayal, loss, or whatever storms life may bring.

Foreword

Rene Hood and I have been close friends for a number of decades. Of all the women I know who are in ministry; no one carries more respect with me than Rene. I watched while she went through trials of her faith that would have put the majority of people completely out of the arena, but not Rene. When I would call to encourage her during her bout with Lupus, she was the one who encouraged and spurred me on. Most people use the scriptures to find comfort; Rene used them to change her circumstances. My hat is off to this modern day Deborah who never quit in her fight, not only to live, but to lift Jesus higher for the entire world to behold.

Being successful in a modeling career at a young age still couldn't quiet the emptiness and loneliness Rene felt. She was running from a secret in her past and with the best the world had to offer at her fingertips, she knew there still had to be something more. God had much bigger plans. This is her journey from a challenging childhood—to the military for a stint in Germany—and on into a powerhouse ministry. This is a must-read if you struggle with a fatal diagnosis, with an inner torment from a memory in the past or if you just can't find the answer to your emptiness . . . Adamantly refusing to be a victim, Rene will tell you how she overcame with scriptures and how you can do the same to overcome your past.

Rene's moment by moment fight against a death sentence as her entire body began to shut down, the internal haunting of Satan's secret blow when she was fifteen and her triumphant climb to victory will leave you unable to put her book down until you have read the last page. What a mighty God we serve!

How faithful He is! From the grips of hell in her physical body to a nationwide ministry of spreading God's love is a story you will not want to miss.

Peggy Joyce Ruth
Author Psalm 91: God's Umbrella of Protection

Apostle Rene Hood has honored me with the opportunity to write this forward to her book. It is at once an honor and a privilege because it is exciting to see God rising up bold women-of-God like her in this current age, who realize and respond to the characteristic of having been sent. Like those apostles of Biblical times, she has a keen sense of purpose and destiny—a focus on fulfilling a divine commission. Because God has allowed me to learn about His character and know Him in a personal way, it is then amazing that He has allowed me to meet this woman who truly exemplifies His character, and get to know her in a personal way. She knows she is authorized to carry out His mission, so she indeed lives as His Word calls us to do: "in Him" she moves, breathes, and has her very being. So, the book's title "Being Found in Him" is aptly representative of her walk—she flows with Him in victory as she stands in her Apostolic Office to execute the affairs of governments.

I am in an excellent position to provide this view of Apostle Hood because I have been privileged to sit at her feet and to observe and learn first-hand how she moves and flows in her Apostolic Mantle and Administrative Offices. During that time, He called me to be a Minister-in-Training (MIT) under her much anointed tutelage. In this role, I often found myself in "awe" of how she seemed able to yield herself to so many concurrent assignments while keeping her peace and achieving excellent outcomes. It was soon revealed to me that she was not doing these things in her own strength; rather, these were supernatural accomplishments by God through her, because of her faith and obedience to Him, and because of her call to the fivefold ministry, she has a greater dimension of the Holy Spirit's anointing in these gifts to which she is called.

Her obedience to God continues to accomplish His work both nationally and abroad. One outstanding example of how God uses this woman was during her tenure in Bellevue, NE when she was called to serve His children here. With the Holy Spirit as her guide, and a determination to glorify Him in a much-needed five-fold Ministry here, she was never swayed by the number of people, or the extent of their respective conditions. Instead, it was the apparent need in each individual (and even their representative families) that energized

Apostle Hood to prayerfully yield herself to God's guidance, and allow Him to build His church through her. That is how the Bellevue, NE Office of The Root of Jesse Covenant Church was launched.

This outstanding woman of God, using whatever resources available, organized, managed, and ministered to the following ministries: Children's, Youth, Priesthood for Men, Destiny-Empowered-Women (DEW); Marriage; Choir; Newsletter; Usher Board; Counseling; Sound; Administration and Training; Church Board, Budget/Finance, Technical, as well as Pastoral. It amazes me, even at this writing, when I think of her involvements and natural leadership in each and all of these ministries; because I can recall that she was anointed, not only to provide marriage counseling to engaged couples, but there was one couple to whom she offered her gifts of altering the marriage gown and designing the wedding invitations! She had to have burned the midnight oil to accomplish all these things, but it still had to be supernatural because she always looked refreshed and always offered a very encouraging spirit; and could always be faithfully found "in position" (Whether it was at the altar during scheduled intercessory prayer or in the pulpit for Sunday or Wednesday Services, or even serving tea at the DEW Fellowship Meetings). I continue to be thankful for the fact that I witnessed all my children come back into the church under her ministry.

It may be hard to believe that while accomplishing all those things, she was still simultaneously used of God for other ministries. These included traveling overseas (during which time she ensured her congregation was covered by other ministers) as well as out-of-state prison-ministry workshops, and foster-parenting teen girls, usually two and three at-a-time. I can recall a photo she took with two of the girls in which they all wore basketball jerseys. Yes, she even played basketball with them!

I believe God is, and has been, making a very strong statement through this life of Apostle Rene Hood—a statement of His power to heal and forgive. Hers is a life that, against all odds, has accomplished the will of God by outstanding faith and stewardship. This book is a glowing report of how "God will take the foolish things to confound the wise." Where society, cultural mores and norms, medical doctors' reports, etc. have counted her down and out, God has said, "she will live and prosper, and be in health, even as her soul prospers."

Read her book and decide whose report you'll believe. It even includes photos and medical records (for those who may need to "stick a finger in the nail-scarred hands" of Jesus . . .). Because of the extraordinary account of this one woman, I am confident you'll believe "the report of the Lord" as set forth in the following pages—and you'll be ever-blessed because of it.

~MIT Valerie P. Pleasant

Introduction

It was a beautiful summer day. The sun had not risen as of yet, but dad was preparing to go fishing. He went into the room where my mother was resting to ask if she needed him to stay home. My mother replied to him, "Go fishing. It's okay; the baby isn't coming today."

Dad proceeded to prepare for his fishing trip, and by 5:00 AM, he was off to Solomon Island. Mom got out of bed; she was always cleaning and cooking. It was not uncommon for the family to wake fresh baked biscuits in the oven. She would start her day early doing laundry, and before her children woke, the laundry would be hung on the line and breakfast would be on the table. On this particular Saturday morning, my mother was doing what she did best—taking care of her family. My two oldest sisters, Mary Louise and D. Lennette, were sound asleep.

Two years earlier, in 1957, my mother had given birth to my brother Lester. Lester lived a week before the angels escorted him home. My grandmother and other elderly people had told my mother that he was not going to live. He wasn't ill or sickly. They said, "He was so beautiful." They believed that he was an angel and that he could not stay here on the earth. (This is what I was told). My mother was hurt from the experience, but she kept her faith in God.

Now, two years later, God was blessing my mother with another child. On Saturday, July 4, 1959, around 8:00 AM, my mother's water burst. Dad was fishing, so the landlord of the apartment building took my mom to the hospital while another neighbor kept my siblings at their home. I have to mention that the landlord was pretty nervous because I was trying my best to get here. My mom said that he would look at her and say, "Don't have that baby yet!"

As he pulled up to the emergency entrance at Freeman Memorial hospital in Washington D.C., the staff came out to assist. As they placed my mother on the hospital bed for preparation, I came out! When I asked her later what my doctor's name was, she said, "It was God."

I was born with purpose, and God let it be known from the beginning. The next day, when the nurse came in to the room to ask Mommy my name, she replied, "Her name is Eureka." The nurse was upset! She really was. She told her that the name meant "I found you." Mommy just lay there quietly, and sometime later she said that the Lord spoke to her and said, "Name her Rene' Gloria."

From the beginning of my journey in this world, God's hands have held me. I did not understand His divine purpose, but even as a little girl I sensed and desired to know what was beyond the clouds. When I turned my life over to Him, He showed me.

As He named me, so I am. Rene' Gloria means *Reborn in Glory.*

> *A good name is rather to be chosen than great riches,*
> *and loving favor rather than silver and gold.*
> Proverbs 22:1

This book is written as a witness of God's faithfulness. He has given us power over all the power of the enemy. My words may be bold, and they may sound as if I think that I am the only child that God has. This is not the case. On the contrary, I tell my story and sing my song that it might encourage you to do the same. God loves all of us and desires the richest relationship with us.

Come and dwell with me at our Father's house, for His banner over us is LOVE.

Chapter 1

Where Art Thou?

*And they heard the voice of the Lord God walking in
the garden in the cool of the day and Adam and his
wife hid themselves from the presence of the Lord God
amongst the trees of the garden.
And the Lord God called unto Adam and said unto
him, "Where art thou?"
And he said, "I heard thy voice in the garden, and I
was afraid, because I was naked; and I hid myself."*
Genesis 3:8-9

It is stated above that they heard the voice of God walking in the garden and hid from His presence. We also learned that they hid because someone told them that they were naked. We can also conclude from this statement that Adam and Eve felt that the proper response to nakedness was to hide it. There is so much that can be said about this statement. I will discuss in more detail in the next chapter.

Adam was placed in the garden to have and to preserve the "Quality of Life."

When Adam fell into sin, he lost his anointing. His anointing allowed the vegetation to grow freely. Read what God said in Genesis 3:17-19. I've added my comments in parentheses after the biblical quotes.

Adam, you have lost your anointing. You have no more power over the ground (the ground from which you were taken). The ground is cursed (including you), your quality of life, you have forfeited, things will begin to grow up that will decrease life (thorns and thistles). You shall eat the herbs of the field. (I believe God was speaking of bitter herbs.) Since you did not choose quality of life, life (sweat) shall continually come out of you until you return to the dust.

The enemy told Eve that she was inadequate and that she needed that piece of fruit to become adequate. She believed that lie and shared it with her husband. As part of the deception, Adam was told that he was naked and that it was inappropriate to stand before God that way. So he hid himself and brought his wife into hiding with him.

Are you where God last met you? When He comes walking in the cool of the day to commune with you, will he find you behind a tree?

The enemy came into the garden God had placed me in and began to tell me that God had forsaken me. He told me that God would no longer meet me at the place He had appointed and that I was alone. He told me I should just accept that God did not mean the things He had said to me; God was only stringing me along.

In reply to the words of the enemy I said, "God, here I am!" You do not have to ask, "Rene' where art thou?" I said, "God, here I am, I'm right here! I'm standing on your word where you left me. I'm not going anywhere. I'm not changing position, and I'm not entertaining the enemy."

I told the Lord, "God I did not know anything about having a relationship with you. God, you drew me to Christ, and then Christ introduced me to the Father. You started this, and you promised me some things in your Word and I believed them. God, I'm not going anywhere! When you come looking for me, you will find me where you placed me." I looked up to the heavens, and I repeatedly said, "I am here! God I'm here standing on your word. When you come, this is where I will be. You will not have to say, 'Where art thou?' I will be right here standing on your WORD!"

Where are you today as you read this book? Are you standing on His Word? Are you counting Him faithful who has promised; or are you accepting the words of a stranger? Stand on the word of God, for He promises in Matthew 7:24-25 that if you build your house on the rock, the storm will not destroy it.

Chapter 2

Nakedness

(Exposure because of the removal of a covering)

*He said, "I heard the sound of you [walking] in the
Garden, and was afraid because I was naked
and I hid myself."*

Genesis 3:10

I am so glad that we do not have to be afraid! What is nakedness?
Is it not the exposure of something; or plainly stated, the emotional
consequences of your actions?

Neither Adam nor Eve's day to day experiences in the garden, or
their nakedness, brought them shame. Only after eating from the tree
of knowledge of good and evil did they begin to feel shame. What
made them feel shame? What was it they now possessed from the fruit
(or their actions) that they had not possessed before? The answer is
knowledge! However, knowledge is not enough.

Paul says in I Corinthians 8:1b, *"knowledge puffeth up, but
charity edifies."* The enemy coerced Adam and Eve into believing that
knowledge alone would be the answer. Genesis 3:6 says:

*And when the woman saw that the tree was good for
food, and that it was pleasant to the eyes, and a tree (to
be desired) to make one wise, she took of the fruit thereof,
and did eat, and gave also unto her husband with her;
and he did eat.*

4

She took the fruit with a desire to become wise. She and her husband were filled with a lot of knowledge without any wisdom with which to apply it and no understanding to rightly divide it.

They had knowledge of good and evil. They now understood that evil and good was present. What they did not have was the wisdom to deal with the new knowledge, nor had they received understanding in how to judge the two. So they felt shame! Shame because they had not enhanced their situation, but on the contrary, had broken their trust with God.

Proverbs 4:5-7 (KJV) says:

> *5Get wisdom, get understanding; forget it not; neither decline from the words of my mouth. 6Forsake her not, and she shall preserve thee: love her, and she shall keep thee. 7Wisdom is the principal thing; therefore get wisdom: and with all thy getting, get understanding.*

Adam and Eve judged their situation as only they could because they had not finished their education—which took place during the cool of the day and in the presence of God. They had decided their situation was hopeless and they resorted to hiding. In the moments of knowledge they shared before God's visit, they had rationalized the hopelessness of their situation, and concluded God would render their situation helpless also.

From that point on, their knowledge continued to spiral downward into shame. Their disobedience led to knowledge they were not able to process; and in their shame, Adam and Eve ran, hid, and began the blame game.

We make mistakes through arrogance and through ignorance. This sometimes happens to us all. When it does, however, acknowledge you've done so. Don't wait to see if God will eventually seek you out. Run to Him! Don't be afraid, don't be shamed. Run to Him in your nakedness and be restored. Allow Him to re-robe you in righteousness and then sit there and learn wisdom and get understanding so that you might apply knowledge.

Even the word of God agrees with this revelation. I Corinthians 13:9 says, "*For we know in part, and we prophesy in part.*"

God gave men a temporary covering while man dealt with their sin and began to understand it and the consequences of it. We now have been given a permanent covering through our covenant relationship/atonement—by the Blood of the Lamb.

Aren't you glad that we no longer have to carry shame? Shame is a very painful feeling caused by guilt, embarrassment, unworthiness, or disgrace. Shame brings dishonor and condemnation. But thanks be to the Lord that it is written in Romans 8:1(KJV): "*There is therefore now **no** condemnation to them which are in Christ Jesus, who walk not after the flesh, but after the Spirit.*"

Let us stand on His word with our nakedness and accept His robe of righteousness.

Chapter 3

"The Attack"

The thief cometh not, but for to steal, and to kill,
and to destroy . . .

John 10:10

The attack began in January 1997, I remember driving from the airport in Dallas thinking and praying about the certain activities at Maryland Correctional Institution for Woman (MCIW) where I had just ministered. My hands were getting stiff and very sore as I drove to the house. A couple of days later, I was awakened to intense pain as I turned using my hands. My hands were so tender, and knots had begun to develop on my fingers and joints. I began to inquire of the Lord, "What is this?" They hurt all the time.

About a week after my return from Dallas I was at the church with Dr. David Schum and the Associate Pastor (Tom). I went over, spoke and showed my hands to David. He felt them and said that the condition was called Reynard Phenomenon—a crippling Arthritis. Then Dr. Schum and Tom prayed for me.

When I left the Church later, my spirit was grieved and I was "mad." As I stepped out of the church door and proceeded to the parking lot, my mouth opened and I said, "Devil, I dare you try to cripple me!" I told him that he was a liar and I came against that attack upon my hands in the name of Jesus. I immediately felt a change. I did not have any other problem with my hands throughout that year.

Fast-forward to October 1997, I am returning from a revival feeling exhausted. I had never felt like this before. I thought within myself that

I had just been going too much and I needed a vacation. After a couple of days of experiencing the same feeling of exhaust, I remembered that my last checkup was over two years prior, so I made an appointment for a physical exam. I remember feeling like I wanted to faint during the examination. The staff was troubled about my appearance so they offered me food and did blood work.

At the time, I was still working in dentistry. I managed to get up that next day and go to work. Sometime in the afternoon I received a phone call from the clinic. When I answered the phone, the voice on the other end said, "We have gotten your results back from the lab and you need to check yourself into the hospital because **you are dying.**" I replied, "I am not, and I will not!" They went on to tell me why I was dying, but I would not accept their words as **the end of the matter.**

My co-workers were amazed, and Dr. G.(my boss) thought someone had lost their mind. The idea that I was dying was crazy! When I had a moment to think about it, I thought the manner in which the clinic communicated my results was very inappropriate and unprofessional. The young lady that called was not giving up on me though. She knew that my blood work was serious and she needed to get my attention so that something could be done. Within an hour, I received a second call and this time she spoke a little calmer, but she was still adamant that I was dying. She asked me if I would not go and check myself into the hospital, would I go see another doctor? She said that she had called an Internist, Dr. O, and that his office was awaiting my call. To that request I said, "I can do that."

I knew that something was going on within my body, but what exactly I did not know. I had no clue. I continued to feel fatigued and my ability to focus on my job was decreasing, though I had not done anything out of the ordinary such as change my diet. I was just doing what God had called me to do—minister to my family and minister to souls. I was a mother with three children and a husband at the home. I had favor at my job so that I could take off a week here, three days here, whatever was needed for my travels to preach, teach, and counsel across the U.S. Souls were coming to Jesus. People were receiving hope and healing in the revivals whether I was in the prisons or in the churches.

God was opening more doors and I was stepping in them and bringing others with me to assist in the ministry.

Once I called, Dr. O's office got me in immediately. I was told that my body was making too many antibodies, and they were attempting to destroy all foreign objects in my body. Within a week's time, my eyes began to become very sensitive to smells and scents. They began to swell and ache very much, and they would burn constantly until, finally, they began to get a clear gel-like build-up and became infected. After this, my right leg was attacked and fluid began to build-up in my knee to the point that my ability to walk was affected.

By now, it is about March 1998 and I have been placed on medication that causes me to be sleepless at night. (Oh, by the way, I am also in college so I have work, school, home and ministry.) Next, I was not able to eat. I would lie on the couch and just be sick to my stomach. When dinner was ready (I had a great cook as a husband) I would end up with my head on the table because I just had no desire or energy to eat food. It was really horrible! By this time, both of my hands are consistently swollen, as well as my right knee and my eyes. Almost daily I kept a fever, had chills and nose bleeds.

I could hardly get out of bed, but I would make my way to the living room and make every attempt to pull down those strongholds. I told the devil to whom I belong and that I trusted God.

Believe it or not, while going through all of this I continued to fulfill my engagements. I remember the first day of a Revival, one of the ushers came over to me and asked me if I was okay. She said that I looked bad. I also remember one of the members of the Church came to me a different day and asked me if I thought that maybe I should stop ministering. I told him that God hadn't told me to stop.

The next week Jacob Kurien ministered at the Church. Though he did not know what was happening, he laid his hand on me and began to prophesy to me. Some of the words were:

> *My daughter, do not listen to the people. I need you to*
> *be like a horse. A race horse. Guard your faith, your eyes*
> *and ears. Every time the enemy sees you he roars against*
> *you. You are taking too many people from darkness and*

bringing them to my kingdom. You will have one battle after another and each will be more severe than the other . . . .

So you see, I had a lot to look forward to! (lol)

At an engagement in New Castle, Delaware, I sat in the Pastor's office before going to the pulpit. While waiting I told the Lord, "I feel like nothing, I have no strength, and your people are out there." I reminded Him of a prophesy He gave me and I stood on it and took that service by faith. The whole revival was supernatural.

While my dad and I were returning from the revival I became even sicker. It was still very hard for me to eat; I got a fever and my hands began to stiffen and ache. I did not share this with my dad. I had to trust God and press on.

After returning home, I became photosensitive and my doctor told me to stay out of the sun. On Father's Day we all went out to eat, and the next day my face was huge! My eyes were so swollen that they were almost shut. I had a face full of dark blemishes. The blemishes were also on my hands, fingers and elbows. I told people that I looked like an ugly bull frog. When I went in to see Dr. O and removed my glasses he said, "What have you done to yourself?" He sent me to the Rheumatologist and he confirmed that I had become hyper-sensitive to the sun. I was then sent to a Dermatologist who gave me creams to put on before the sun block and recommended certain fruits.

It is July now, and I am eating less and less but I am gaining weight. I am looking like I am about seven months pregnant and stay with nausea and fever. My girlfriend flew from Washington D.C. to spend two weeks with me for my birthday on July 4th, but I was not able to entertain. My condition continued to worsen, and I was back and forth from the doctors. I am given more medication, but nothing is working.

Chapter 4

The Cool of the Day

And they heard the voice of the Lord God walking
in the garden
In the cool of the day
Genesis 3: 8 (KJV)

Do you realize that God doesn't try to carry on a conversation with us in heated moments? He comes in the cool of the day.

As I was writing a letter for one of our ministries, Destiny Empowered Women (DEW), God began to lead me to break down the meaning and purpose of the dew. As I began to search it out, I learned that dew is water droplets condensed from the air onto cool surfaces—a process that usually happens at night. Then I pondered and considered why the dew would fall at night and why upon a cool surface.

When I think of dew, I think of women. We learn and love to refresh others—it's a part of our makeup. Sometimes in our zeal to refresh, we try to water and cause restoration before the cool of the day. We see someone in need, but their temperament isn't right to receive. We try to pour it in them anyhow. When the person becomes frustrated and reacts in an ill manner, we are puzzled by their response. The answer to this dilemma is that you did not allow the dew to fall on a cool surface. When dew falls on a heated surface, it immediately evaporates. Therefore, the dew was not profitable. It did not fulfill what it was sent out to do.

11

The Lord, in His wisdom, did not come to Adam and Eve in the heat of the day when they were preoccupied with methods of cooling off (such as resting under a shaded tree, or while they were taking a swim). He came to them when the temperament of the day was perfect for learning.

In the stillness of the night the Lord would approach me and give me wisdom and understanding. When the surface was cool to allow the dew to sit upon it and gradually soak in. When there was nothing else moving around—just quietness, stillness and rest.

Just as the earth rests from a day of work and is renewed by the dew, so are we by our cool-of-the-day visit from the Lord. Wait on them. Expect them. And run to Him as you hear His voice walking toward you to commune with you.

Chapter 5

I Will Believe the Report of the Lord

*Who hath believed our report? And to whom is the arm
of the Lord revealed?
Surely he hath borne our grief, and carried our sorrows:
Yet we did esteem him stricken, smitten of God,
and afflicted.
But he was wounded for our transgressions; he was
bruised for our iniquities:
The chastisement of our peace was upon him; and with
his stripes we are healed.*

Isaiah 53: 1, 4-5 (KJV)

As the attack continued, I found myself unable to lie down at night
in bed without choking. I informed my doctor, and he told me that it
would pass. I knew by then that he was confused and didn't know what
to do. He kept telling me that my body had to adjust to the medication.
Finally, one morning I woke and went to the bathroom and I couldn't
urinate. I called my doctor right then and there and left him a message.
I told him, "You keep telling me that my body needs to adjust to the
medicine. I woke this morning, and I can't urinate. Something is wrong
and it isn't my body not adjusting!" He called me back and told me to
come in. He took some labs and told me that he was setting up an
appointment with a Nephrologist (kidney specialist).

To bring you up to date, my husband is not concerned with what
I am going through. He could not deal with it, and he wasn't dealing
with it. The appointment Dr. O made with the nephrologists was two

hours away in Temple, Texas; and my husband said he did not know how I was going to get there. My daughter, who had just graduated from high school, had to take me. Just for clarification, I had not done anything wrong to him for his lack of concern. As a matter of fact, he told the pastor that I was a wonderful mother, wife, homemaker, and kept a clean house. He told him that he just could not deal with me being sick. I remember one particular day we had just driven up in the truck and parked under the carport. We had been visiting a neighbor who had recently gotten out of the hospital. I remember it like it was yesterday. We pulled up in the drive and my husband turned the truck off. I said to him, "Why is it that you will cook for our friends, visit with them, and show compassion, and here I am your wife, battling illness and you treat me as if you do not even care?" He turned and looked at me and said, "You are tough and you'll be alright!" The response was not that of one speaking faith; but on the contrary, it was spoken with anger and resentment.

For years I had to deal with verbal abuse, whether he was criticizing the size of my breast in front of the children or just trying to belittle me with his words. It did not matter the time of day, nor was there a motivation factor. I will share more in other chapters.

It is now July 27, 1998 and I am on my way to see the Nephrologists in Temple, Texas. This was possibly the longest ride I have ever taken in my life. I hurt whenever my daughter went over a bump. I had to put my car seat in the farthest laid-back position. It felt as if it was an eternity and that I was spending it in hell because I felt so miserable.

I did not have any strength within my natural being. My temple (body) appeared to be decaying rapidly. I struggled to bathe myself and it was an even harder chore to wash out the tub. When I went to the bathroom while waiting to be called by the specialist, a nurse came in and wanted to get a wheel chair. I am walking like someone who is about to give up the ghost at any moment. I also had the appearance of a seven-month pregnant woman because of the severe swelling.

My daughter was in the room with me while I was being examined by the specialist. After examining me for approximately ten minutes, he sat down and told me to sit down by his desk. This doctor looked at me and said, "I thought this was going to be easy after talking to Dr.

O, but I give you three months, and you are just going to go 'poof'."
I said, "Excuse me?" He said, "You will suffer, be in pain, and you will
be gone."

I looked at him and he looked at my daughter, then returning to
me, he pointed his finger toward my daughter and said, "She is big
enough, she can fend for herself." I looked back at him, I felt no fear.
I was vexed! I could not believe that he said that in front of my child
whether he believed it or not. I told him that I did not believe that my
daughter was ready to give me up and that I was not ready to give my
children up. He walked out the door and I grasped my daughter's left
leg and looked her straight in the eyes. I told her that her mother was
not going anywhere. That's what the doctor says and not what God
says.

I still believed the report of the Lord!

I was admitted that day, and for two days I was unconscious most
of the time. On the third day, I asked God for leadership. I needed
to know what I should allow and what I should not allow. They had
replaced my IV site four times in two days because the medication was
burning my veins. When I told the nurse she said that "it was suppose
to burn" in a very nasty tone! The next time my nurse came in to give
me medication in the IV, I refused it and the battle was on.

Chapter 6

Yea, Though I Walk Through the Valley . . .

Of the shadow of death, I will fear no evil;
for thou art with me;
Thy rod and thy staff they comfort me.

Psalm 23:4

The night before I was hospitalized I could not sleep. I hoped for tomorrow because I was in so much pain. As my husband and children slept, I laid on my bathroom floor in the fetal position. As I lay there, my body made a puddle of sweat beneath me, my skin became grayish in color and I felt the agony of my soul. I felt so all alone—It was such an agony that I could feel a horror of darkness. I felt unloved and unwanted by my husband; and surely I would not use my children and bring fear within their hearts. I could not share my pain with my parents because they would not be able to stand with me in faith. So in the darkness of my soul, I reached out through the thick darkness for the light.

I remember telling God, "Lord I hurt so bad . . . so very bad and I know that I could just give up the ghost (meaning the spirit) and come home. I know that I can, but there are people out there that do not know you and they are my assignment. I am to take the gospel to them. Lord though I hurt, I trust you. (These words were breathless and said in blind faith) I know that I am in the valley of the shadow of death. I will not quit on you. I will not give up. I can't do this though, I need your help. I know that this will only give me more compassion and make me more longsuffering. God, I am trusting you. I will not fear evil because I know that you are with me."

I made my peace that night and set my intentions while laying there on the floor and I chose life.

Now, I am in the hospital and it is still the third day. After refusing the medication in my IV, the head nurse came in on the a.m. shift and ordered the medication in the form of a suppository. I remind you that I had been complaining since day one and three IV sites had been destroyed because they had continued to give me the medication intravenously.

When I was admitted: I had swollen eyes; swollen glands with tenderness; I was unable to eat; I had severe nausea; and fluid building in my abdomen. It was very hard to walk because of weakness, muscle pain in my arms, waist, joints, and especially my right shoulder. My right lung was giving me problems because of fluid. I experienced abdominal pain (even from motion), fever (it was nothing to have 103-105 temperature), low blood pressure, high pulse, etc. I had a "death sentence" upon me, but I was not accepting it. I understood that I was no longer under the law, nor was I under the curse of it.

He anointed my head with oil in the presence of my enemy . . .

For the first three days of my hospitalization I was told that my condition was caused by a bacterium and that they needed to draw the fluid from my abdomen. That wasn't comfortable and they had to do it more than once. In a couple of days the medical staff was baffled because the fluid came back clear. So around the fifth or sixth day they needed a needle biopsy of my kidney because I was in renal failure. They took me down and put me under for the biopsy. I do not know how long I was out but when I woke, I awakened to an instrument inside of me and with mega pain going up and down my leg. All I could do was to tighten my jaw and repeat the name of "Jesus" and ask for help.

The doctor, acknowledging I was now conscious, informed me that I still had too much fluid in me and that he had not been able to retrieve the kidney sample. He actually said that he was going to try again (while I was awake!) and if it didn't work, he would send me upstairs and they would have to do the biopsy openly at another time. I will show you hospital records in later chapters to confirm my conditions and certain happenings. By the way, when he tried again I was still conscious and it did not feel good at all. Needless to say, he wasn't able to get the biopsy that day.

On the seventh day, they took me back down to do an open biopsy through my back. I now have a nice five inch scar to confirm this. The results were in on day eight. The head doctor walked in with his "posse" in my words. He never came to see me alone. There were always other doctors with him because he needed their opinions. My case had been puzzling and they were trying to keep me from dying. (This is their confession and not mine) I was told on that day that my kidneys were a **four** which is the worst of kidney diseases. I was also told that they needed to treat me with Cyclophosphsmide. I was informed that this drug would make me sterile, that it would knock out my immune system, that it would cause me to become bald, and that I would also get diarrhea. These were just a few of the side effects from this form of chemical therapy. The head doctor stated that these symptoms were not all that would happen but they were the ones I would probably be most concerned with.

I had just turned 39 years old on July 4th and there I was in the hospital and the doctors had given me no hope of returning home to my family. My daughter had just graduated from high school and she was afraid to leave home for college in fear of receiving a call from someone informing her that her mother had died. My son was in junior high school and I wanted to see him finish school and become a strong, respectable man of God.

When the doctors left my room I turned my head to the window to look out. I recited what the doctors had said to me unto the Almighty God: "Lord, they said that I will never leave this hospital. I will never have a productive life, and I will not be able to do the things I once enjoyed. I will be this way for the rest of my life, and if I am released, that I may need to come to the hospital once a week or more for treatment."

We all know that the devil is the father of lies . . .

With tears flowing down my eyes, I spoke to the Lord in the fetal position because of the continuous discomfort and pain that raged in my body. "Lord I know that you hear me. I know that you have not forsaken me. I also know I could say, 'why me?' I have been living by grace, and you have strengthened me to walk upright before you. I have been traveling across the U.S. doing what you have told me to do. I know that you hear me." About that time my faith rose up and I said, "I know right now that you are looking down here (I could see Him) and you are leaning to the right, speaking to Jesus as you point to me. You are saying: '*See her, do you see her? She is walking through the valley of the shadow of death, but she knows, I am with her.*'"

I could actually see this taking place in the heavens. Right after that, God spoke to me from the book of Isaiah. He spoke from Isaiah 43, 44 and 45. He did not speak with a still small voice, but when He spoke, I heard thunder, the sea roaring and power. He began to say how He had formed Jacob with purpose and cause, and that He was God and besides Him, there is no God. He comforted me with the truth of His word, and despite all that I was feeling I knew that I would come through.

My daughter had remained with me in the hospital and she was much afraid. With all that I had to deal with, I also needed to encourage her—trying to persuade her to get out of the hospital, and enjoy her friends that had come to visit. She stayed right there. I was her "Pride and Joy" she said and she wasn't leaving me. I did get her to go out for a couple of hours, but I know where her heart was all the time.

As I think back, I cannot grasp the tensions, stress, nor the frustration and agony she must have felt. For her, I was all that she had. She had graduated with honors, the world was her canvas and she was the artist. Within a fraction of time, her canvas held no inspiration; her focus was lost; and her heart was filled with fear. She was there for me and I was fighting the good fight of faith to ensure her of God's faithfulness.

I remember when I had her, when I held her in my hands and she gave me so much joy! I wanted to hold her with my faith, right there in the hospital, and ensure her that her mom would be right there with her to share her dreams and ambitions.

Chapter 7

We wrestle not against flesh & Blood . . .

But against principalities, against powers, against the rulers of the darkness of this world- against spiritual wickedness in high places.

Ephesians 6:12

I told you earlier that my husband did not want to deal with this matter. We had came home one day after visiting a friend that was ill and I asked him why he was willing to go here and there to visit others and to offer prayer, but wasn't a bit concerned with me. He told me that I was tough, and that I would be alright and then he got out of the truck. He did not offer me comforting words. As a matter of fact, he would know that I wasn't feeling well and could not do for myself and he would leave me to go to a basketball game two hours away. What do you say to something like that? If I needed immediate attention, I wasn't getting it from him. He didn't show me any kind of compassion or care. He did not want to accept that I was in the condition that I was and that he was the reason (in part) behind this attack.

I guess you are probably saying, how was he the reason? Some of you may not accept that curses are real. I am living proof that they are. Let me move slowly as I explain. My husband had been married previously—his first wife died. My husband was born in Port Arthur, Texas. He was from French descendants and his family and friends practice dark arts. They dealt with those principalities and spiritual wickedness in high places. Now when I married him, I wasn't aware of this. You'd better know the generational curses that your intended spouse has on his/her life and make sure that they are dealt with prior to you two becoming one. I'm saying this because if you don't, it could cost you your life!

As I was saying, his first wife died. And from the information I could gather, she just fell sick, the doctor never could diagnosis the cause of her illness. She suffered for a year or so, and was gone. I was told that she endured neglect and ill treatment from him as I had. I am thankful that I can look back on my days of perils and **REJOICE** in the Lord my God in the land of the living!

During the time which my husband and I were dating, I lived in Washington, D.C. The summer prior to us being married, he came to D.C. to visit. Prayer is so very vital and sensitivity to the Spirit is a must! I remember he had been there for a few days, but on this day we also got a surprise visit from another relative. The enemy knows how to camouflage the truth. This particular relative was known to associate with darkness. During her visit, I had lain down to take a nap and while I was sleeping. I felt a thick shadow crawl upon my bed and then upon me as it began to press against me. I knew that it was a spiritual attack and as I wrestled to speak, I was able to say the blood of Jesus and it disappeared. I accredited the incident to the presence of my relative because I did not stop to ask the Lord, I just assumed. I know that we have so many demands upon us from day to day, but we have to quiet our minds and allow the clarity of the spirit to speak to us and **even the more** when we are in spiritual warfare.

Within the first year of our marriage the attacks began. My husband got up at 5 A.M. to prepare and to leave for work. After his departure, I would feel something crawl on my bed and it would begin to try to suffocate me. I would try to plead the blood of Jesus and sometimes I would have to wrestle with that spirit for what appeared to be several minutes to become free to speak out.

This continued for months. He would leave and some dark spirit would immediately begin to harass me. I could feel the darkness and the fear that was associated with it. I remember one morning turning from the window toward the door and as I opened my eyes, there was a spirit leaning against my wall. It appeared as a male around the age of sixty with a cigarette in his mouth. He was puffing the cigarette and blowing out the smoke as he looked upon me. His appearance was jaundice in color. I remember not feeling threatened, but tired, so I went back to sleep. Before falling back to sleep, I did say "I'm not afraid of you." I knew that he wanted to intimidate me, but I felt the comfort of God's Spirit, so I rested in his defense.

I am reminded of another day—I was lying in the bed with the pillows supporting my back and my blanket covering me, reading my bible. I heard what sounded to be my son calling my name. Up until this time, I was feeling great and all of a sudden, I began to feel as if I had a virus with a high fever. I heard the voice call out and say "momma!" I turned and looked to my right to answer what I thought was the voice of my son, only to see a spirit that appeared in the bodily form of him. It had the height, size and shape of him, but there was a strange or weirdness in his appearance. Within seconds of this appearance, I began to feel sick! I felt as though I had a very high fever, I had begun to feel as though I was drooling and it begun to feel as if I had chills associated with the fever. Let me say, that it truly felt real! This is why we cannot accept what we feel as our reality. We cannot accept it! We must at all times know the truth, believe the truth, speak the truth out audibly and establish it before your enemy!

As I laid there in the bed wondering what in the world was going on I said within my mind, "God I am not sick and I am not drooling." As I attempted to rise up my left hand to touch my mouth, an unseen force offered resistance. I knew that I wasn't sick, but under attack! My confirmation was to touch my face, to prove that this was all an illusion of the enemy. I knew that I could not have been drooling. There was no reason for this feeling down the side of my mouth. The enemy wanted me to believe this lie and he was making a good show of it. Again, I attempted to reach my face, but this time within my mind, I began to call on the Lord because the enemy was also pressing against my mouth so that I could not speak audibly.

As I prayed my hand began to move gradually towards the left side of my face and when I finally over powered the forces of darkness and felt the side of my mouth, the touch confirmed my suspicions. I wasn't ill! I also knew that this image which appeared in my bedroom wasn't my son, so I spoke with a loud voice and said *"The blood of Jesus!"* The spirit just appeared to burst! It seemed to burst into little droplets of spirits and leave in many directions. As I write this, I am reminded of the word of God which says: "*The Lord shall cause thine enemies that rise up against thee to be smitten before thy face; they shall come out against thee one way, and flee before thee seven ways.* (Deuteronomy 28:7)

I am a living witness that He meant all that He said and He makes good on all His promises. God is faithful who has promise . . . .

I can give you so many more examples of spiritual warfare in my life that I have actually seen with my own two eyes. I will give this last testimony and then get to the point of my statement earlier about my husband being the reason. Instead of using the word reason, let me clarify my statement by saying, the curse or assignment was against him, but I was the object of desire. I will explain in more details very soon, bear with me.

Once again, the alarm clock rang at 5 A.M., and he prepared and left for work. As I think on the manner in which these attacks happened, I have come to conclude that those demonic spirits were just hanging around in my home waiting for the moment in which they could attack and their moment was normally early in the morning mainly after the departure of my husband.

On this particular day, the spirit of darkness appeared again in the shape of a man, but not as any man I had known. The spirit climbed on top of me and then began to press against my body. I can see it as if it is happening presently. I feel that spirit holding my hands and yet at the same time, smothering my vocal cords to prevent me from speaking. As I acknowledged what was taking place (by this time, I had been under attack for months—close to a year) I realized that my natural and mental being was exhausted. I truly had no energy whatsoever to defend myself from my opponent at this time.

I know within his thoughts, he considered himself the victor. He had gotten me to a place and it appeared that I was helpless. This was his day of victory! After sleepless nights and restless days, I found myself with no natural strength and a mind that was fatigued too!

There had been days when I refused to rest because all I had to look forward to were battles. Though the majority of the battles happened early in the morning, I also dealt with them throughout the day when I tried to nap because of the lack of sleep during the early morning hours. They were constant and they were intense. They began to take so much out of me and I was continually warring throughout the day in prayers for the victory and for it all to be over. I was feeling that these attacks would never end. I vividly recall laying there on my back and saying these words within my mind, "Holy Ghost I can't do this! I have no fight within myself. (I couldn't speak and I had no strength to release his hold from my vocal cords) I need for you to fight for me."

Right there before my eyes . . . . Hallelujah!

He is Jehovah Nissi (my banner)!
He is Jehovah Shalom (my peace)!
He really is Jehovah Shammah (my abiding presence)!
He is the great "I AM" He is . . . .

I saw the Spirit of God (which had taken its abode in me) rise up and grasp both hands of this dark spirit and began to lift him off of me. That was an awesome, supernatural experience! I saw the Spirit of God that was sent in Jesus' name defeating the enemy for me. It was unbelievable! I felt as John did, these are the things that I saw and experienced because of the Christ and I must tell it that others might believe and that the believer might continue in the faith.

Chapter 8

He is the True and Living God and He is Almighty!

Let me take a moment to point out that unconsciously I had thought within myself that my strength had assisted me in my triumph over my enemy again and again. God never needed my help. I am so amazed at the fact that when we are truly helpless the greatest results are manifested. I said unconsciously because in all of the previous testimony, I called on the name of Jesus and knew that by His name the enemy was defeated. But somewhere in the back of my mind, I was also aloof to the thought that because I had a certain amount of energy the enemy was defeated. This was truly an "Arsenio Hall—Ah hah" moment; it was something to think about.

Before going to the hospital, I spoke to my Pastor and he said that he had been praying and the Lord told him that I hadn't done anything. He was looking for answers and so was I. I went to Dr. David Schum's office one day and we decided that we would both fast and pray to get an answer to what was happening. We had planned to meet back at his office in a few days. I believe that it was on the second day of my fast when I received a word from the Lord. He said that it was a curse on my husband.

He went on to say that his first wife died because she didn't have faith and I was alive because of my faith. A couple of days later I went in to meet with David in his office. He greeted me and began to talk about a few things as he examined me. Sometimes the answer that you get from God may trouble you and cause you to hesitate when the time comes for you to share what He has spoken to you. I was about to go and David walked away from me and said, "Rene' by any chance could this be a curse from Stanley." I replied, "David that is just what God told me." Then he proceeded to say that God told him that my husband's first wife died because she did not have faith and I was here because of my faith. I was blown away! It was actually the same exact words spoken to me by the Lord and I knew that it was true.

A few days later, my husband and I were in the same area in the house. I was sitting at the table and he was cooking. I asked him if it was possible that maybe someone there in Port Arthur had liked him and he did not reciprocate the same feelings and they cursed him by cursing the woman that he loves and marries. He looked at me and said, "Why does it have to be from me?" I reminded him that he was brought up around those who entertained familiar spirits. I also reminded him that the black arts were practiced around him, even among his friends and relatives.

About a year later I had a luncheon at my home with a couple from the church. The discussion came up about my attack and they said that they were praying for me and the Lord spoke to them and said that it was a curse from my husband. I smiled and then shared with them what the Lord had revealed to me and Dr. Schum.

Another Testimony:

The enemy will use anyone who will open himself or herself up to him. I was working in dentistry as an assistant and I was great at what I did! Whether I was removing a temporary crown from the patient, preparing the tooth for the permanent crown; or making a temporary for a patient, my work was anointed. I had known that my co-worker only pretended to be my friend. On one particular day, she could not restrain herself. We were in the lab and she looked and me and said, "I am glad that you can't perform like you once could." I looked at her and I felt sorrow. She felt such low self-esteem that she would use an opportunity like this to kick someone. I walked away and by the Grace of God I said Lord I forgive her. I had told the Lord prior to that that I forgive my husband for treating me like less than a human being, and surely not as his wife. I had seen people treat dogs they did not care for better than the treatment I was receiving. It hurt deeply coming from both of them. I truly realized that my battle wasn't with them. I thought to myself they would have to deal with their actions and I need to **keep my eyes on the Lord.**

The enemy is alive and powerful and he will use his power against the children of God. So please put on the whole armor of God each day that you may be able to withstand in the evil day, and having done all STAND! (Ephesians 6:13) And remember to always stand on God's word. It will not return to the Lord void. It will do that which it has been sent out to do. (Isaiah 55:11) Trust God and watch him destroy principalities, powers, rulers of darkness and spiritual wickedness in high places!

Chapter 9

Come . . . .

And Peter answered Him and said "Lord, if it be thou,
bid me come unto thee on the water." And He said,
"Come."
And when Peter was come down out of the ship, he
walked on the water, to go to Jesus.
Matthew 14:28-29

In circumstances we sometimes ask "Lord is that you?" And when it is, He answers and tells us that we can do the impossible. Jesus announced to the disciples that they did not have to fear, it is I. Peter, understanding that Jesus was walking on the water (which was impossible to do) said to Jesus if that is truly you; bid me to come! Peter understood that if Jesus bid him to come (to do the impossible), that all of creation had to yield its strength to help him succeed. That is why the waters held him up, that is why the wind became his banister. The word was sent out and whatever assistance Peter needed to get to Jesus was provided. Peter began to sink because he no longer wanted to walk on water <u>because</u> of his present circumstances.

So many times we are called to come . . . to come up in our relationship with the Lord and we look round about at our situation and we talk ourselves out of it because we deem it impossible. Jesus was saying to them all, "Look at me. As I am, so are you. Come out of the boat and experience the power of the Almighty.

It is now day eight in the hospital, and I am told that a mass has been discovered on my liver. They told me that before I can be treated for my kidney, a liver biopsy is needed. The nurse arrived to take me downstairs. She realizes that my IV has been in for four days and decides that it needs to be replaced. She checks and finds that it is working properly. She still wants to remove it because of the length of time it has been in that vein. I ask her not to remove it and fill her in on the whys. She would not go to confirm my statement; instead she removed the IV and attempted to find another site to no avail. She then takes me downstairs, un-prepped and left me there. When the doctor came in, he noticed that I did not have an IV and called for one to be placed. After about twenty minutes he said that there wasn't anyone available. He went and got a sonogram machine to find a vein and attempted to set it himself. He stated that a vein had been found, proceeded to do something and left. All of this time, I am still in my bed (I was wheeled down in my bed). After a few minutes, I turned to my daughter and said, "My arm is aching." She replies, "Mom that man knew that he had missed your vein when all that blood shot out!" I wasn't looking at him. I had been looking at her all this time. I laid there in pain as my arm went into spasms and we waited for someone to return.

He finally returned with a nurse. I told him that my arm was hurting and he told the nurse to check the site. He had missed the vein and hit a nerve. They had to send me back upstairs to my room and give me something for my arm. When I returned to my floor, the nurses came out to meet me and to apologize. They said that they had never seen so many mistakes done to one individual.

I understood exactly what was going on and I continued to pray and ask the Lord for wisdom. I felt as though a dark cloud was over me and I knew that an assignment of death had been placed upon me by the devil himself. I wasn't afraid and I did not withdraw from my journey with Jesus. My journey was to accomplish the impossible through Christ Jesus! When Jesus called Peter out of the boat without saying it, He said, "Will you trust me?" That is where I was at that moment. More things were wrong than they were right. Almost everything the medical staff did up to that time appeared to be working against me and it was discomforting.

On the ninth day, they tried to set-up a new IV, but they could not. My body was tired and my veins had collapsed. One of the doctors told me that my heart was not pumping any blood. That my blood count was dropping very low and I believe they wanted me to accept blood. Once again in the fetal position, dealing with the pain making itself known in my body, I spoke quietly to them and said that I am tired and my body is tired, just leave us alone and we will be alright. I could only say that because I knew who held my life in His hand.

All of this time they are still doing other tests with machines. To my surprise, my husband came to visit. Yes, this is the first time he came and the last. He came in and picked up the newspaper, my son came over and kissed and greeted me. After my son's greeting, my husband decided to kiss me, sit down and read the paper. My son (Coffey, which was from his first marriage) sat beside me and we talked for about thirty minutes. Then my husband told me that they needed to go to the mall and they left. I truly could not focus on his inability to come to terms with this. I had to give that to Jesus because it would have caused me to lose my focus and my life.

By the eleventh day, they still had not been able to establish an IV site and they could not move forward without the IV. The head doctor was getting a little perturbed with me. He had sent a psychologist up to see me a few days earlier and informed her that I was depressed. After her examination of me she stated that she would be recommending a second session only if I felt that I needed to talk to her. She stated that I was not depressed. I felt loved and had a strong foundation in faith. She said there wasn't any indication of depression though I was dealing with so much at the time. The head doctor did not like that because prior to her visit, he told me that he could give me something for depression. I informed him that I understood that he has accessibility to many drugs that assist many people in different ways, but I did not need a drug, his prescription could not help me through my spiritual battle.

One of the doctors that I saw when I first was admitted was a Christian and he would come in and tell me to be strong. I appreciated that. We were talking one day and he was explaining what was happening to me. He said that my body was making a whole lot of antibodies and they were fighting against my body and not realizing it. He said they were not seeing my body members as members, but as aliens and were trying to destroy them. Trust me, I felt the warfare! I told him that I respected him and what he had learned. I was thankful for him, but I said, "I am in spiritual warfare and you don't understand."

I saw what I was going through as the body of Christ. So many times we are used to destroy each other. The members of the body of Christ are used as the enemy's antibodies to silence the words of truth, to dim the light, to rob us of our joy and strength, and in so many other ways. He uses members of the same body to destroy itself. They believe that they are doing God's service by ridding the body from enemies while all the time, they are incapable of discerning the members. Therefore, they begin to create havoc, destruction, and much pain. I pray that I will always be sensitive to the Spirit of God and the members of the body of Christ so that I might show love and not cause harm. There are not words to describe the emotional and mental anguish that accompanies the betrayal of one's members whether consciously or unconsciously, the pain is still afflicted.

Dear God, I pray with a broken heart and a sincere soul that the people that are called by your name alone will seek with me a consciousness toward you and your children. We all are so different in so many ways, but we all are family. Help us to see each other as you see us and to love each other as you love us without respect of persons. Your love is there for us unconditionally, help us to accept your image and likeness in our life so that we might seek to give and be a blessing to one another . . . In Christ name I pray, Amen.

The head doctor came to see me on the eleventh day saying that I needed to allow them to place an IV on my heart or neck because they could not find any more sites to use on my arms. He said that I still needed the liver biopsy. I asked him did he really expect me to allow that doctor who was the cause of my arm going into spasms after trying to start an IV to cut on my liver! I informed him that I realized that he could make a wrong incision and I could bleed to death. He told me that the doctor was known for having the gentlest hands in the world. I told him that I didn't agree. There was also the protein that my kidney was throwing out into my abdomen which would cause the procedure to be more difficult. I was told that because of all the fluid the doctor would have to go through my stomach instead of my back. Oh, how I thank God for the blood of Jesus. So many things I would have had to endure had it not been for my redemption. Needless to say, I did not allow them to place the IV, nor would I consent to the doctor doing the liver biopsy.

The head doctor left the room with the other doctors that assisted him with my case and he wasn't happy with me at all. He said that he would allow me to rest that day and he would be back in the morning.

Some people say, "What a difference a day makes." It made no difference to or for me! When I informed the head doctor the next day that I had not changed my mind, he leaned back against the wall, and in front of his assistants, he began to let me have it. My daughter was sitting to the right of my bed and this was right after breakfast. He told me that I needed to allow them to drug me up and do what they wanted to do with me because if I didn't, I would not see Christmas. It is August at this time. I stopped him from speaking, looked at my daughter and asked her if she okay. She replied yes, so I told him to continue. He went on pronouncing my death. Then he told me that he would give me about thirty minutes and I needed to call him at his office so that he could set up everything for me to have the biopsy (and whatever else they deemed necessary) the next day.

When he walked out of the room, my daughter looked at me and said, "Mom, what are you going to do?" I looked at De'Nina and I said, "You are going to help me get up from this bed and you are going to help me shower and **I am** going to walk down there with this walker to the nurse's station and I will tell them to call their god up (speaking of the head doctor) and I am going to tell him that they are not going to kill me because I am going home." That is what I did! After being there for twelve days, I had them give me paperwork to sign myself out.

Now the Lord had spoken to me a few days prior and said, "When you leave, don't go home because there is not love there." I called my Pastors and told them what God had said and they confirmed that I did not need to go there. I went to my parents' home. As my daughter drove me out of that city, I began to feel better. I had felt this heavy black cloud over me at the hospital and I knew that it wasn't the plan of the enemy for me to ever leave the hospital. But there I was alive and leaving the hospital. All I had was the report of the Lord which stated *by His stripes I was healed* (Isaiah 53:5) and that He sent His word to heal me. I felt the Lord call me, as He called Peter, to experience the impossible. I stepped out in faith with all of my focus on His promise. There were circumstances surrounding me and it appeared that there was nothing available to hold me up or sustain me in this storm. But I kept my eyes on Him who had commanded me by His word and through faith to come . . .

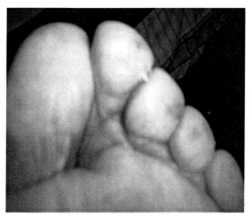

Left foot: The effect of cold winter (Reynard Phenomenon)

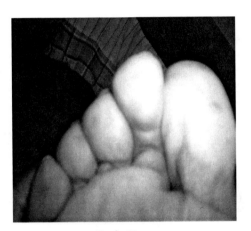

Right Foot

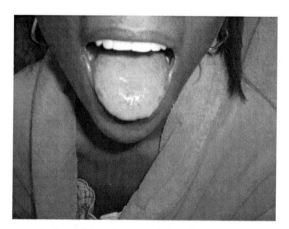

Dark markings began to blemish my tongue

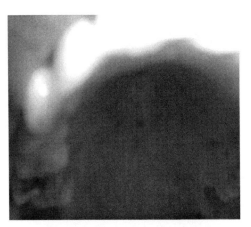

And the roof of my mouth

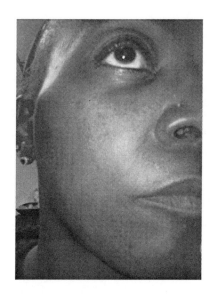

Chapter 10

Greater is He that is in me . . .

Ye are of God, little children, and have overcome them:
Because greater is He that is in you,
Than he that is in the world.

I John 4:4

When I left the hospital, things did not get better though I felt relieved. It was one battle after another one. Please know that God's grace truly was sufficient.

I arrived home to my parents' house on a Thursday and that night I had a few dreams. In the first dream I was in my house and as I looked out from the living room window, our yard was filled with weeds and they had also filled the living room. I turned to my husband and said, "We have to do something." But he turned and walked away from me. I began to pull up the weeds one after another and as I did, I remember thinking that I would need a big trash bag for all of this. I do not remember how long it took but all of a sudden, as I stood in the room, all I saw was a green tender plant. It was so tender and it appeared to yield to the wind.

As I observed the room, everywhere I looked was clean. The floor was wooded but it was polished and clean. All of a sudden my clothes changed and I had this long white dress on and I began to dance, praising and worshiping God. It was so awesome! I was lost in Him. For how long I don't know, but it was splendid. As I continued to dance, my husband came back in the room and looked at everything with this stone look. He attempted to take me as his wife but he could not. There appeared to be an invisible barrier between us. I remember looking at him and he was so stiff, he could not even bend his knees.

Then the scene changed. I was walking and a man appeared from out of nowhere with a huge animal on a leash. Actually the animal looked like a very ancient wolf with the mixture of a bear. Its color was a grayish-black. It looked very old, it was very large and it walked on all four legs. The man walked with the animal on a leash that was a very thick and heavy chain. The animal was very horrifying. As I walked down the street they followed me. When I no longer saw them and turned a corner or crossed the street, they were there. The man asked me something and I became very irritated with them. All of a sudden the animal became a man and another man appeared with what looked like an old ice cream truck that had the door on the side. When the door was opened, smoke ascended from it. At this time I was not watching and I fainted. The man with the truck tells the man that was once the animal to drain me (to remove my strength from me), but something disallows him.

I also have another dream that same night (August 1998). In this dream there is a gigantic wheel ascending and descending from the sky. It came down and I got on. Someone else was already on the wheel and as it began to ascend, I knew I needed to get off at a certain place. I also noticed there was not much to hold on to, but I was able to maintain my grasp. The other person wasn't sure where he needed to get off, but somehow I knew and was able to assist him.

I am explaining it like this because the wheel did not stop for us; it was as if we were supposed to know our stop. The person that I assisted joined other people as they stood facing forward before a throne and they all had military uniforms on. They stood at attention and they were given gold metals as I watched. I never saw the face of the person that gave them their metals, nor did I see the face of the individual to the right of him. As I turned to walk away, the person that gave the medals to the people reached out his hand with a glass of water in it and gave it to me. I remember wanting to stay and thought to myself, "Why didn't I get a metal?" Later, I realized that my battle wasn't finished. As a matter of fact, it was just getting heated up and I am thankful for the refreshment from the Lord. I did not and I still do not understand the fullness of these things that I experienced, but I felt the need to share some of these things with you nevertheless.

As I continue to fight a good warfare I know that I truly encounter the same kind of spiritual attack I experienced from that animal in my dream that desired to have my life. But as in the dream, so was the reality. God said "NO!"

I am still at my parents' house and the drama continues. My primary doctor was out of town when I decided to sign myself out of the hospital and I'm sure you can image that he was not happy when he got the news. I gather that he called my home and was informed that I was at my parents' house. I remember sitting on the right side of the bed as I raised the phone to my ear. Dr. O had a sincere voice and he asked me, in so many words, "Why are you out of the hospital? Do you not know that you are dying?" Now I remind you that I am not feeling that great. My body is still doing whatever it wishes to do whenever it decides to do it and I'm feeling all of the pain from it warring against itself.

I can truly take this lesson I have learned about the members fighting against each other and apply it to the members of Christ. How many times do we not recognize one another? How many times do we war against each other causing damage and I do mean serious damage. Damage, that takes years to repair because we did not recognize a member of the body of Christ. Instead we have created antibodies and we try to destroy them. We tried to destroy them because they didn't look the way we wanted them to look or sound the way we wanted them to sound. Most of the time, it was just because of ignorance. So what that it may be a weaker member, it's still a member. And if it is a weaker member, it will take even longer for restoration.

Back to the phone call, I'm listening and this man is saying that I am dying. Why does everyone keep saying that? Are they all trying to get me to concede that this is a true statement? With the phone in my right hand against my right ear I told Dr. O that I did not believe that. I remember that he kind of stumbled for words as if he was caught off guard and had to regroup. He stated that he did not have all of the reports from the doctors at the hospital, but he knew that my kidneys were in renal failure, I had a mass on my liver and that they needed to do a biopsy of my liver prior to treating my kidney. So in his mind, I was placing myself in harm's way. He was very adamant about what he thought and what the other doctors had said. I told Dr. O that I was not dying. He said, "That's what the doctors are stating." I told him that they were liars! I really did! I said that they do not speak the truth. He stated that he would get the other reports and call me back. He also asked me if I would come in and see him.

I told him that what he was saying was the report of man and I will not accept it. I also told him that I would consider coming back in to see him. He had tried to persuade me to go back to the hospital, but I told him that I would not do that. I told him that those men were trying to kill me. After realizing that his words were not causing any change in my protest, he quietly said that he would call me in a couple of days and check on me and we said goodbye.

I must say here that I do thank God for Dr. O. He was passionate and sincere. He meant well according to his studies of the internal body. He just did not have a clue at the time that what was being manifested in this earthly body was not natural. On the contrary, it was a force that one could not see with the natural eyes. He worked with me patiently feeling that he was not getting through to me and only he knew the fear he felt when I would not follow his instructions. I could not at the time focus on what he felt or did not feel. I could only focus on what I knew to be true and that was *greater is he that is in me than he that is in the world.*

At that moment in my life I was like David and there was Goliath ranting and raging saying that he would cut off my head and feed my carcass to the fowls of the air and to the beasts of the fields. There I am, a mutt in his sight. I'm just an irritation to him and it would be better for him and his army if he destroys me now in front of all them sitting around hearing him rant. I did not have a speech memorized nor had I stood before a giant before. All I knew is that he had declared war. He had declared that I was not worthy to live and that he would be the one that would personally annihilate me. I took that personal! Yes I did, I took it personal because all that he was saying to me was contradictory to what God had been telling me since he saved me in 1978.

Somebody was lying and the truth was not in them. So I had to take a stand of faith. I was sure that I had built upon the rock. I had attained security and assurance by the blood of the Lamb and I wasn't giving up what God had declared to me without a fight. So it was on.

With "who I am" and what I had been taught, I surely ran with the little strength that I had against that giant that attempted to keep me from my **destiny**. All I had was the word and that is what I aimed with. I allowed the word to proceed out of my mouth and when I did, the winds from heaven assisted me. As I released the rock (word) from my hands, a south wind of the presence of the Lord came from behind and fortified the power of my release. Once I released the rock, I found myself positioned on my knees. When I looked up I noticed that my enemy had fallen down. I had to continue to act. I could not allow him to rise up. With the presence of the Lord empowering me, I got to him who wished to destroy me. As I looked upon him I saw his hatred and strong desire to end my life. With the leadership of the Holy Spirit, I took up the sword and it strengthened me as nothing ever had before. In a silent moment without hesitation, I lifted up that sword, tilted my head and from the left side of my face and with all the hope that had been given me I swung it. As I had believed and expected, the head of my enemy laid beside him.

Death had sought after me. It had called out my name. It wanted me as a trophy to display to weaken and intimidate others. I fought for the kingdom of God. For all that He had conveyed to me over the years. I fought for all of them that I had shared the gospel with so that they might know that God was real, true, and faithful.

Prophecy given **4/25/99** about picking up some more rocks (stones) . . .

The Lord said, "My daughter, you are constantly in a battle. When one battle is over, another one is on its way. When the one battle is over, the new one is more severe than the one over which you have already had victory because I have called you and chosen you to be a fighter. There is no easy way out. It is a constant battle. Many people are looking at you and they are mistaken about you. Doubts may creep up, but your heart is right with me. No one knows your heart but me. No one can enter your heart and see, but I am the one who looks deep inside your heart."

"But expect more battles ahead of you. More battles, but you do not have to fight alone. It is not the battle for survivors, but it is a heavenly battle. It's a spiritual battle. Every time the enemy sees you, he comes against you with a more fierce battle, but don't be afraid. **The one that is in you is greater than the one that is in the world.** And through you, I will change and deliver many people from the power of darkness and you will transfer them unto my kingdom. I have chosen you to be a soul winner. A soul winner in my kingdom! As you continue to win souls, I am going to promote you spiritually and you are going to train many others to take the yoke, the yoke together."

"But as I promote you, I want you to continually keep on humbling yourself, keep on humbling, keep on abasing yourself and say 'God I have done nothing.' As long as you say, 'I am nobody,' I will make somebody out of you for my Glory. **So get ready to pick up more smooth stones** because there are more Goliaths, one after another waiting on you. Have more smooth stones in your sling to fight against them and you shall not be defeated. I'll give you victory. The end result will be victory, says God. Whatever the enemy tries to steal from you, I shall replenish back to you, to your bossom; at 30, 60 and 100 fold. When I replenish back to you, you shall put it into my kingdom for my glory . . ."

People out there, who feel that the battles will never end, don't give up! God is faithful. There may not be an easy way out, but there is a way out. Just stay consistent in your walk with Him.

Prophecy given 12/12/99:

"You know the Lord says that there is nothing too hard. But you are in a battle; you have warfare ahead of you. You have already been in a battle. But every time you have been in a battle, I give you victory. Ahead of you, you have to fight more. The enemy is roaring at you. He's coming against you with a gnashing of teeth because he's losing people from his kingdom. But I say unto you, **that greater is He that**

is in you than he that is in the world. Don't look at the situation because the devil tried to bring the people that are close to you to turn against you. But I say unto you, it's only my Grace. I am going to touch more lives, more hard-hearted lives, hard-like-a-rock hearts so stubborn. Through you, I am going to melt them. Bring them into my kingdom. But always be submissive, be humble, be submissive to authority, so I can promote you."

I do pray that this prophecy will be a blessing to you. In a storm we normally can't see the person right beside us and we project to ourselves that we are all alone. You are never alone. God not only knows your name, He knows before you go through what you are about to go through. He is so faithful. He cares about us so much. He doesn't want any of us to fail. We are winners. Through Christ we have become more than conquerors. Remember that no matter the storm, situation or circumstances, He has equipped you for glory. When you feel that you can't take another step, that your strength has left you, His Grace will empower you and cause you to do the impossible.

Greater is He that is in you than he that is in the world!

Hopefully this prophecy will be extra special to those fighting illness—illness that will not let go of its hold. It appears that when you believe you have a breakthrough something else arises. Just hold on to His hands for there is help in His hands.

Prophecy given 2/23/2003:

The Lord said, "My daughter, it's not easy and it has never been easy because you have gone through thorns. You have walked through thorns and bristles. It's only by my Grace your feet did not get hurt. I put new shoes on you, new shoes. Otherwise you would have gotten hurt.

I make your forehead like the forehead of a flint. I made this special cord for you. It is tougher. You will be able to stand the wiles of the enemy. I want you to know that arrows, one after another, from your own people, from your past, one after another tried to hurt you, but

I am the Lord your God. I have been your refuge and your dwelling place. Because I am a shield for you, those arrows did not hurt you."

"I am a healer. Everything that came your way is like an arrow that struck against your heart. Sometimes it was so hard for you to take it, but I am a shield around you."

"I say unto you today, keep your integrity. Be loyal to me. I will use you. I never promised this is going to be easy. But in the midst of tribulations and trials, I made you a winner and I will make you a winner. Don't look at the past. Do not look at the present situations. If you look at it, it is hurting; it will hurt you more. Keep your eyes focused on me. I am the Lord your God and have called you with an everlasting calling. I do not repent of my calling. Keep your eyes focused on me, and then you shall not go down. I will bless you materially and financially and you shall be a blessing to many spiritually said God."

Some of the prophecies are not grammatically correct but I have typed them as close to verbatim as they were given to me. Again I hope that they will enlighten you to the assurance of God's Grace and Mercy. He will never leave you alone.

There have been a many days when I felt that God was anywhere but with me. I did not feel Him when I prayed. I did not see His hand in my circumstances. All I could do was to encourage myself in the Lord by bringing to remembrance His words. I still did not see nor did I feel, but I *hoped*, and *expected* to see the salvation of my King manifested before my enemies.

Chapter 11

Settlement vs. Entitlement

It is so easy to accept a settlement in a battle

I have been out of the hospital for more than six months now and I am still seeing the Internist. At this moment I can't recall totally why I needed to go in on this particular day, but I believe it had to do with dry eyes and swelling. I do remember that it was a beautiful sunny day. I went to Dr. O's office and I was given a prescription to get filled for my eyes. After waiting a significant amount of time, I was called to the pharmacist counter and told that I no longer had coverage for my medication.

In August of 1998 when I had returned home from my visit to the Nephrologist, I was greeted with certified papers from my now ex-husband's lawyer because he had filed for a divorce. Accepting that he did not desire to stand with me through this battle, I offered no resistance toward his request. I did not understand it, but I accepted it and prayed to God as I set my heart to maintain its focus upon the Lord. The divorce was granted December 1998 and we had spoken concerning my health insurance which was covered by his plan. It did not cost him a penny to maintain my coverage and he told me that he would keep it. Needless to say, on the above mentioned day I realized that I am no longer with any kind of medical coverage. I have been diagnosed with a crippling and deathly disease that demanded at this time some form of medication, lab work, and other tests. I went back to the office and to ensure that our conversation was private, I communicated with him on the phone in the darkroom (where the x-rays were developed). Still having a sense of humor, after the greeting I said to him, "By chance did you cancel my health insurance?"

Without any concern or any degree of understanding of what his actions detailed he answered and said, "I figured you could get your own coverage." I am sooooo appreciative of God's love and peace because a smile actually came upon my face while a soft and tender revelation swept across my mind. I tilted my head in the dark toward the receiver and said that you cannot get coverage for a preexisting condition with a new policy. He couldn't care less. I was no longer his wife by his own decision. I felt that a mutt with fleas and no master was shown more love and consideration then I had been. I remember telling him that I needed to go. I walked into my operatory and looked out of the full glass wall and I indentified my enemy which was fear/devil and said that everything that appears to come up against me I will use as a stepping stone toward developing a greater relationship with the Lord. I said out loud and audibly, "This too will work for my good. I will not fear because I do not have medical coverage, Lord I give you this situation. I am not depending on the coverage, but I am depending on you." I told the Lord that I knew He was aware of this prior to my awareness of it. I said, "You already have a plan and I am going to trust you no matter what."

I remember my body aching and my temperature rising to somewhere around 103 degrees. God and His Holy Spirit being my witness, I found my way into the bathroom and began to speak over my body. I told my body that I knew that it was tired and hurting, but I needed it to work. I told my body that it had the peace of Jesus flowing through it. I trusted each member of my body to work together with joy, peace and in harmony. Then I began to run in place, lifting my legs up as high as I could stimulating my heart as works of my faith as I encouraged myself in the Lord.

I could have accepted what my ex-husband said as the end of the situation. I could have said, "I have tried and tried and here again to no avail." I understood that day more as these events were unfolding that I was given a promise by my "Creator" who loved me with an unconditional love. He wanted the opportunities to show me of His love and Grace. I remembered that it was written in the word of God:

before I pray, He knows what I have need of (Matthew 6:8). All I was doing was remaining on His word as I told Him I would be.

The word of God had told me that I had an inheritance through Christ Jesus. It said that my inheritance had no limitations or boundaries, that all I had to do was believe and that I would receive. I want you to know that with everything that I was, I knew that this situation was going to work for my good; and that when everything was said and done that I would see the manifestation of the promise spoken in II Peter 1: 3, *"According to his divine power, he hath given unto us all things that pertain unto life and godliness, through the knowledge of him that hath called us to glory and virtue."*

Everything that we need is provided for us at any minute. We were not created in His image and likeness to receive a settlement. We were created in His image and likeness to receive our entitlement as children of God. Can you imagine a father that lights up the world with a magnitude of colors and sounds waves each time you acknowledge him? I hear Him rejoicing over me continually as I would over my children as I held them near me to ensure them of my care for them.

I can't be any clearer on this matter; you do not have to settle no matter how long the battle appears to be. If you are tired and feel as if you have nothing more to give, position yourself in the fetal position. This represents your inability and your willingness to submit to the plan of God which is the natural course of life that was intended from the beginning.

Chapter 12

The Fetal Position;
place of empowerment!

Here I am . . . It is total darkness! I know that there is life all around me, as a matter of fact; I can feel it flowing through me. Yet, at this very moment, breathing is difficult for me. I can feel the darkness as it surrounds every part of my being, but I know that it is well. There is a peace that generates from the center of my soul.

I remember when I was living in Washington D.C. and I had a dream that I was in this gross darkness. As I continued to walk forward, I repeatedly said, "I know that you are with me, I know that there is light." It seems like the more I walked the darker my surroundings became. At one point it felt as if the darkness would suffocate me. But as I continued, I found that eventually I arrived to a place of light.

Each one of us, at some place on our journey (I would like for you to think of journey as stages of development) find ourselves at a passage of darkness. I've been there and I'm here even as I write this section.

When my body was consumed with pain, I would position myself in the fetal position. Did this position relieve the physical distress of my body? No, I cannot say that it did. Did it bring comfort to the mind, the chatter box of my being? Did it somehow restore peace to the emotions? What is so wonderful about this position that each child without being instructed knows to position themselves in this way for their birthing? As I said, my body still felt pain and discomfort once I got into this position. What it felt even more, though, was centered. There was a profound quietness and stillness that resonated from my very being when I got into this position. The ache was there and it was intense, but its intensity could not drown out the "presence of knowing." There is something so powerful about the fetal position because it takes you to a place of knowing—right there in the dark!

The fetal position whispers to you, "This is where you belong. This is for your good. You don't have the understanding to see all the different activities that are going on around you, but you wait . . ."

I was in the dark at that moment! I knew that I was headed precisely in the right direction though I had no idea where I was going or when I would arrive. As a matter of fact, as soon as I tilted my head by raising my crown toward the indicated direction and tucked my chin as a sign of submission, the darkness became harsh. It felt as if it earnestly sought after me with purpose and desire.

That thought made me ponder . . . This place of darkness, as in my dream, is another journey. There are characteristics being formed within me at this very moment that will enable me to fulfill my destiny. Though I cannot see in this place of darkness, I can feel my heart pounding as new life surges within it. There is wisdom in all of this though it feels like madness.

When I had my son, I had arrived at the hospital, my water had burst, and I became fully dilated in a very short time. As my doctor felt my stomach, she noticed that the baby had not gotten into the birthing position. She ordered a sonogram that revealed that he was lying on his back and had his head up looking toward me. Needless to say, he was in no position to participate in his birth.

I believe that we are empowered in so many ways when we participate in our births. If we do not participant we will become dependent on others and not exercise our talents. I'm in that position presently. I feel it as the contraction is causing my heart to race and slightly presents what I would consider shortness of breath. There is really nothing to fear, it's a normal and healthy process. By the way, I am not sharing medical documentation. I hold no medical degree whatsoever. This is spiritual. I'm focused on what is needed for our healthy transformations, births and rebirth in the spirit.

Can you for one moment imagine yourself as that infant? When we walk by a nursery or embrace a newborn in our arms, our minds think such things as: weak, timid, and fragile—and so they are. But they are so much more! Just as the journey from labor to birthing speaks intuitiveness, courage, longsuffering, endurance, determination, and so much more; so do infants. These giants, though disguised in small fragile bodies, have so much wisdom, purity, and love to offer the world they have just entered.

As changes take place in your life and darkness seems to occupy all your mental awareness, know that this is an opportunity for birth. There is something through the years that has developed and it is ready to be birthed. Tuck that chin in, raise your crown in the indicated direction and allow the darkness of the unknown to assist you in working it out.

All that we are and shall ever be is presently within us. We have to be courageous enough to position ourselves in the mannerism of life. Darkness is just a part of the journey; it is not the destination! There has, and will always be LIGHT . . .

Chapter 13

Don't forget to Dance . . .

I hope you never lose your sense of wonder
Never fail to eat, but always keep that hunger
May you never take one simple breath for granted
And when you get the choice to sit it out or dance
I hope you dance . . . -Lee Ann Womack

I thought that I was enjoying my life prior to my attack of illness. I had travelled to other countries and visited many states. I had at that time been volunteering in the penal system for seven years, been to the mission field and done so much to try to make a difference with my life.

When I was told that I only had three months to live, I knew that the statement wasn't true, but it still made me reevaluate my life and to look inward and discern if there was anything I would rather be doing. The answer was yes! My heart cried out for the children of the inmates I was volunteering to assist in the penal system. For years I headed an "Angel Tree" program which was a success. Yet my heart cried out for something more. I needed to feel deeper, to see clearer, and to express myself louder in love and with compassion.

While I was at work one day, my girlfriend Paula, who was a hygienist, said that a friend of her husband was starting a foster care agency and asked had I ever thought of being a foster parent? She thought that it was what I had been looking for. I went and got the documentation about the agency, and before I knew it, I was filling out the application and going to training. We were instructed time and time again that the most important thing to remember is not to *give up* on a child.

For as long as I can remember, I have been a dancer! I enjoy dancing. I love to hear the music and allow it to vibrate in such a way that the vibrations become a part of my being to the point that its rhythm intertwines with my muscular and skeletal system in such a manner that I mimic the sound waves as my body takes on different forms and shapes. Dancing is an awesome form of communication and expression.

Have you ever danced in the rain? With only the rain drops as music. Sounds fill the air as they fall and the language in which they speak is fascinating! It's so incredible that one is swept up in the miraculous . . . There is a oneness as rain runs down your body and yet, some remain upon your flesh. Remember to listen to the music and to participate and **DANCE**!

Chapter 14

The Enemy Does Not Discriminate

He just comes to steal, kill and destroy. From whom and
to who, it matters not.

I would like to speak on these scriptures, and in doing so I would like to share a story or two from the pages of my life. We all have stories, but it is our willingness to share those stories that empowers one another.

My story begins early in life at the age of 15. I was staying at my sister's place for the weekend and had decided to go swimming at their community pool. I enjoyed going because I enjoyed the water and swimming. On this particular day, a gentleman was there who was much older than me. I do not remember having had an in depth conversation with him, but I do remember us meeting and sharing words at the pool. I remember he said that his name was Jay. As a matter of fact, when I left the pool I knew that he was there and that he saw what building I went into at the apartment complex.

I do not know if he was watching the apartment or what. I only know that my sister and her husband went out that night and a short time later there was a knock on the door. It was this man Jay. Being ignorant, naïve, and a poor judge of character, I opened the door only to be taken advantage of by this man.

The rape happened at the end of the summer right after my 15th birthday, and now I am back in school. It is basketball season and I am feeling as if I had lost my dexterity and it had been replaced with clumsiness and a feeling of being overweight. I looked the same, but something strange and mysterious was going on that I wasn't aware of, nor had I experienced before. There I was going on with my life thinking I had been strong and dealt with what was done and that all worries were behind me . . .

A month or so later, I found myself in a very difficult situation. After feeling this weirdness, I discovered I was with child. I had a life within me and I could not be upset at this life that now dwelled within me.

At this point in my life, I am truly lost. I have no one to talk to with whom I could share this dilemma. I am 15 years old, in high school and a man that I do not know has raped me and I am afraid and have nowhere to turn. At this time in my life, I considered my dad my best friend and yet I knew that I could not share this information with him. I normally felt that I was there for him and not him for me.

As for my mother, she had so many burdens upon her that I could not add another one to it. I also knew that she would assume that I had gotten pregnant from being promiscuous. I had this life growing inside of me and I knew that it was a being in me. I would sit up at night and wonder if it was a girl or a boy. I wanted so much to protect this child in ways that I had not been protected. I wanted to care for this child in ways that I felt were lacking in my life. But reality is much crueler than a dream.

I felt honored at the thought of being a mother. I felt even at that age that I would be a great mom. I had experience with children from working with the Roving Leader Program in Washington, DC for two years and I had baby sat for my cousins who were married with children. I was not so much excited as I was protective of this child. One thing I didn't add in the equation was the neighbors.

It was a cold snowy day and I knew that I could not withhold this information any longer. I sat down and I wrote my mother a letter because that was the only way my strength provided. I then went for a long walk so that I would give her enough time to come home, to read it, and let the news settle. I know that I walked from D.C. to the edge of Maryland by the Jumbo, but that didn't matter. I stressed wondering what would happen when I returned home. Would she think that I was a whore? Would I bring dishonor to her? Would she ever trust me again? I didn't know what she would think.

We had a loving relationship at this point. However, my mom did not share with us her lessons on life. She only made rules and expected us to maintain them. She wasn't a bad mother, she only knew to keep us clean, clothed, and fed and she did it by working hard whether at home or on the job. She and my dad were separated at this point and I had felt that she resented my love and adoration for my dad. I understand now what I was discerning and I understand why. At that age and without experience, I could only make it about me.

I finally made it back home with anxiety flowing through my veins from not knowing what to expect. Would I be laid out on the floor as soon as I enter the threshold? Would I no longer be accepted as her child? Tears of fright filled my being and sadness consumed me because of what I had shared with my mother. How could she understand my pain and my fear?

To my surprise, the issues I was concerned with weren't the issues that concerned her. All I could hear ringing in my ears were the words, "What will the neighbors say?!" I heard that repeatedly during the course of her conversation—hers because I was excluded from the conversation. I never heard, "Tell me what happened. How do you feel? You are not alone, I'm right here." I never got a hug to assure me that everything would be alright. I was confronted with the neighbors. My happiness, future, plans and goals were now weighing in the balance on the judgment of the neighbors. The life that I was carrying was now subject to the thoughts and opinions of the neighbors who were not members of the household.

My heart sank deep within me that night and I thought to myself that it was not possible for it to sink any lower, but I was wrong.

A few days later I experienced the greatest devastation I have ever experienced to this day of my life. This day is fuzzy in my mind because of the situation I was confronted with and had to endure. As I remember it, my mother told me that she had made an appointment for me. That we were going to see a doctor concerning my pregnancy. It was a day that the whole world ceased to have motion. There was no light, no wind, no words, all was dark and I was trapped in the darkness. I remember the doctor examining me and confirming that I was with child. Afterward my mom's mouth moved and the word should never be repeated. I was prepped and taken into another room all alone. My mom did not go with me.

I equate this walk with the last mile. I felt as if I was on death row—that my life was about to end and there wasn't a thing that I could do. The room to which I was taken was cold! It offered me no comfort whatsoever. I was placed on a table similar to the one that women have to visit on many occasions for our pap smears. God only knows that I wish that day was my introduction to a pap smear, but it wasn't.

It was my commencement to death! As a young girl, I would sit on the porch and view the world and cry because of the hurt and pain that was afflicted upon mankind by them. I would say to myself "Why would my mom bring me into a world full of so much hurt and pain?" A world overwhelmed with so much sorrow and suffering. I actually ached to the core of my soul being here and I hope to discuss that in the next chapter. Today I was experiencing cruelty on a new level because it was personal, and in effect, opened a door and empowered death over me in such a way that I sought it unconsciously and consciously for years.

They positioned my legs in the holders and then strapped them. I was anesthetized and I believe an IV was started. There was this metal pole that hung to my right and there was a clear cylinder hanging also. I remember the doctor and nurses setting up the equipment and placing tubing in me. I heard a noise, and to this day, my eyes still collect tears as I see my child being sucked out of me as if he or she was dust or dirt on the floor that served no purpose; and therefore, needed to be removed. I saw the life taken from me by a tube because I couldn't protect that life. I felt I was weak, ignorant, and alone. Oh how I wanted to break free and save my child, but I didn't have the strength, experience, or know how.

Sometimes ladies, we just don't know how . . . that isn't our fault.

After the procedures, I was given some instructions concerning what to expect. Are you ready for this? I was then placed in a cab and sent home while my mother went on to work. I'm fifteen years old and I have just been awakened to brutality and inhumanity on the ugliest level I could conceive at that time. The ride home was timeless and yet it was eternal. There was no time; it had stood still so that the pain could continue to rip at my soul without interruption. I was lost, floating in cloud of numbness, consumed with pain. Who could I run to? Who would understand the anguish of my heart, mind, and soul? My head, body and mind ached because of my loss. Did my child judge me? How much pain, if any, did he or she suffer? Would this pain ever cease to gnaw away at me?

I returned to school within the week, but I was never the same. When my siblings were sleeping I would sit on the end of my bed and I would cry. I would talk to my Aunt Maria (she was deceased), to whom I felt closeness, and cry. I would wonder if my child was a boy or a girl. What color would his or her eyes have been? Who would he or she have resembled? There were so many unanswered questions. I wondered if I would ever know peace and understand the madness of men's actions.

On one hand, a man took complete advantage of me. On the other hand, I was comforted by no one! I thought the world was cruel and unmerciful before and now it felt like a total wilderness in which one has to be on the lookout both day and night against vultures of the human race.

I finished that year in school and when the next year started, my counselor informed me that I had enough credits to graduate. I only needed to go to night school to fulfill my English4 class. For me, these words were a gift and a sign of hope. I had withdrawn from activities and a social life. I was still looking for a way out—a way out from the hurt, loss, and shame which had imprisoned me. I was truly lost and I was miserable. It was as if all hope had been crushed and restricted from me in one action. I was now in a world alone, but something on the inside was leading me to a pasture I did not know existed.

Before all the drama in my life began, I had been modeling for Barbizon in Chevy Chase, VA. I had hoped to be an airline stewardess and travel the world. Now I just wanted everything to be alright again. I was working at Gino's on North Capital Street when I graduated and I was a manager, but I needed something else. I so desperately needed to put this episode of my life behind me. So at the age of 16 years old I began to study for the military.

When my mother found out that I was considering going into the Army, she said that I was too young; but I told her that I had to leave. That if I did not leave that I would be messed up. My mother still did not know that I had been raped, only that I had been pregnant. I passed both the physical and academic tests given and I was given the option of leaving on that day or on a delayed entrance. I choose that day because I felt that my life depended upon it.

I soon found out that there was no place to run . . .

After finishing Basic Training, I was stationed at Fort Benjamin Harrison in Indiana. I played basketball for a team on base and played with more determination then I had ever played before. Looking back at those days I wonder if I played to forget or to strengthen myself against the challenges of life. I really had a new attitude and I was resolved to win and take my team to championship. Once we made it to the championship, my determinations deepened and there was no other place for me but in the winner's circle. It was as if a warrior had been awakened within me to fight and be victorious. I was unconsciously condemning myself again and again for not being strong enough to remove myself from that table. I had not planned or realized it, but I had vowed to be strong for myself and others who were weak or unable. This was manifested each time the basketball was placed within my reach or hand. I had to get it in the goal! And I did, for myself and the team.

It is amazing, the power and dexterity that can be demonstrated when a person is running from hurt and pain. I realized that playing basketball with every ounce of my being was causing me to suppress my hurt and pain that I wasn't able to totally resolve or confront at that point in my life.

In the 1800s, Sigmund Freud listed suppression as one of several ego defense mechanisms that manifests after a traumatic incident. There are others in the same professions who have stated similar theories. As for me, it only helped temporarily. After the game I still had the same aches and pains and I could still see the day my child was taken from me.

Chapter 15

Facing the Darkness

*It isn't the outer darkness, but the inner that frightens
us the most!
You can run but you cannot hide . . .*

I completed basic training and AIT and was stationed to Stuttgart,
West Germany working at Patch Barrack as a Financial Specialist. The
job was a great and the hours are fantastic! I had begun modeling there
in Europe and had met several individuals who I considered friends.
They were also coworkers in different departments.

One of my girlfriends (who I will name Phyllis) was also my
roommate and we got along very well. Then there was Daniel (these
are not the true names of the individuals) who had a special interest in
me. He wanted me to be his lady. As a matter of fact, later on in our
relationship he became my fiancé. There was also Billy, a laid-back
kind of guy, who appeared to have my back and watched out for me.
The next person was Alex. He was small in stature, but appeared to
demand respect and a level of loyalty from the other guys. Alex was
dating a German young lady from whom I received much education
concerning the ways and diplomacy of the country. She worked with
me to improve my interaction skills with the people of her country by
adding to the knowledge and language base I received from our "head
start" school on post. She and I had many wonderful days together
exploring the countryside. Last, but not least, there was Dallas.
He was the kind of person who was always trying to fit in, but felt

awkward all the time that he is trying. Besides them, there were others that I hung out with, partied, and had a great time with but the ones I mentioned established a close bond with me and we loved and cared about each other.

This group of people that I described somehow placed me as the center of the circle and adhesive that held us together. They also spoiled me . . . I do not know if part of that was because I was modeling and they wanted to assure their place in my life. Whatever the reason, they were there. I remember verbalizing my want and need for a car. Without exaggerating, I can say that within two weeks there was a Mercedes Benz sitting in front of my dorm and it was mine! I saw a mink one day and declared how nice I thought it was and before I knew it, I was wearing it. The relationship with these people came with great perks and outstanding benefits. And though we did many things that brought laughter and joy, there was still a darkness that haunted me and stole the totality of my peace. I was smiling, but I was empty and unconsciously crying out for help and for a meaning to life. In all of this fun and excitement there was something greatly lacking.

I began to look at my life and what I was doing with it. Why had I made the decisions I had made? Had these decisions been a lifesaver for me or was I still drowning? I had to ask myself, "Am I happy? Have I acquired peace in my heart, mind and soul?" The answer to all of those questions was no! I was as miserable as I was the day I left home. In all honesty, I was actually more miserable because though I had a nice job and good friends, I felt that they did not know me. Even more, I felt that I did not know me. I still felt so lost and alone no matter what gifts and attention I received from others.

So I decided to turn inward. I had to go back to when I was happy and at peace. That took me back to the age of about ten years old. I was a chorus member at Beulah Baptist Church. I was not singing with the choir on this particular day. I was singing from the congregation seating and I was singing "I surrender all—all to Jesus I surrender, all to him I freely give, I will ever love and trust him . . ."

The next thought of happiness took me back to when I was at an elderly neighbor's home helping her out because she was a widow and very lonely. I would spend the night, clean for her, run errands, and just be a companion and a friend (if that is possible at that age—it was). My greater joy was when she would ask me to sing and before I could think I would be singing "Everyday with Jesus."

Chapter 16

The search for "why"

One can become cynical or begin a journey of life . . .

I had become a victim and that is all I knew to be. It was stamped on my forehead and everyone saw it except me. I realize that there is an aroma that seeps through the pores of men and women who have been traumatized and neglect to deal with it within their cave and cages of despair. A lot of us smile because we still want to love and share love, but we continue to be spotted by the leeches—individuals whose purpose is to get over and to take from others because they are not willing to do the work themselves.

There were two soldiers in my barracks that sniffed me out. They would always have some "hard luck" story and be in need. They were a part of the "can I borrow" gang. They borrowed, but never paid you back; yet they'd come back for another loan and you'd give it to them. Was this my way of trying to help, hoping to find comfort for myself? It felt as though I was trapped in a cycle of being played the fool. Let's get taken advantage of again or be a sucker! Everywhere I looked in my life, someone wanted from me and it did not matter that I was hurting and needed to be healed. There were head hunters after me and I needed to find a place of safety.

I began to search for that peace by starting with the only person I had known it with—God Almighty. Instead of going to lunch with my friends, I would find myself sitting in front of the piano in the chapel crying out from the depth of my soul without words but with tears and sincerity. My heart was aching and I needed answers to be given that would liberate my tormented soul. When I did find words to say, they appeared to be worthless, words such as: "I don't know what to say, but I would like to know and understand you along with your reasoning for me being born." At this point in my life I still had not figured out the purpose of mankind, I thought that we (human beings) stole, killed, and destroyed.

I had been writing my mother throughout my military experience, but my words to her were things of no meaning to me. We discussed the activities happening on the base and my trips to the different towns. We'd maybe talk about a promotion or other family members, but we did not discuss the deep wound that continued to bleed within my heart, mind, and soul. I knew that it was consuming me and that I needed someone bigger than me and my situation to help me.

So I continued to find myself at the chapel. I wasn't seeking the Chaplain on duty, but why I did not seek him out, I do not know. Maybe because he was a male and that is where all of my troubles began. I was being drawn to someone who would not hurt me, nor disappoint me. When I sat there at the piano and cried out with or without words, I felt a presence. Someone was there for me. I could not see this person, but he was there and I wanted to know what I needed to do to have a relationship with him.

Chapter 17

A Time of Separation

*"Wherefore come out from among them, and be ye
separate," said the Lord. And touch not the unclean
thing; and I will receive you.*

2 Corinthians 6:17

It was during this time that I had a dream concerning the Lord's desire
for me. There was nothing different on this night from any other. I had
prepared for bed and I slept—

I woke outside on the side walk looking up because of the sound
of the trumpets! As I stared toward the heavens, the clouds began to
separate and creatures I had never seen before began to descend upon
the earth. At the precise moment that the clouds began to divide, the
earth began to burn. There was fire everywhere and I did not know
what to do. As I considered the matter, the earth began to shift and
the scenery changed. I was placed on a mountain and the fire could
be seen in every direction. People were crying, screaming, and trying
to climb up to safety. At one period in the dream, people were trying
to push me into the fire and when they did, one creature after another
would grab them and drop them into it. This went on for a long period
and I thought that I was experiencing the end of creation and we all
were lost.

I became horrified as one of the creatures grabbed me with their
claws. My thoughts were, "I'm a goner," but instead of being thrown
into the fire, we began a flight around the city. To my surprise, the
area to which I am being taken was not on fire. We arrived to a

certain area and the creature began his descent until my feet touch the sidewalk. As I looked around, it became apparent that I was standing in front of a club at which I had recently been a winner of a dance contest. Before I could consider the reasoning for this journey a huge hole appeared in the wall of the building of which I was standing in front and I was able to see within. It was also apparent that the people inside were not able to see us. As I looked into this club I saw drunkenness, lust on the level of adultery and fornication, rudeness, and many other things. While viewing all of this, there was a strong, authoritative but calming voice speaking to me saying how these actions displeased him.

It seemed as if I was there all night witnessing sexual harassment, lying, cheating, lust, words I would not choose to utter from these lips. I was not partaking of this, but I could feel all of it as if I was—probably because I had associated with them in many of the acts seen though I was not a drinker, smoker, drug user, or permissive. I was a sinner and I was vain.

Those women I saw that night reflected me. They were concerned with what they had on and the way their hair fell to the side or stood on top of their heads. They wanted to know that when they walked in the room, the hounds would pick up their scent and begin to circle them. Little did they know that they were setting themselves up for disappointments, delusions, lies, and heartaches. But this was the norm; it was the way in which women had been conditioned to accept validation. Now there was a gentle but stern voice speaking to me saying that these attributes were not acceptable or becoming to his creation.

As the voice was acknowledged and received, I was convicted of my lifestyle and knew that many changes were ahead for me. What they were and how they were to be accomplished I had no idea, but I knew that I was willing to take the journey if given the chance.

Afterward, I was again taken by the creature and we were in flight. As we journeyed, I could still see burning throughout the world. As we began to descend toward the dorm, I could see the agony upon many faces and their distress. Was this the end for us all? Why had I been shown the misery and deception of sin?

As this heavenly creature placed me upon my bed, the very moment my foot touched it, the flames ceased to burn in the earth for as far as I could see.

Why was I shown these things? What was I supposed to do with this information? I was not sure, but I began to inquire the very next day. I commenced to withdraw from my friends and to invest time in reading the Word of God and trying to be still so that I might hear him again. I examined my life and activities and took the initiative to remove all things I thought would be offensive to the Father I had heard and wanted to know.

Within the next month, I had stopped modeling, removed myself from the social life I shared with my friends, and basically became what some would call a hermit. I went to work and when I got off, I hit my knees and read the word. Sometimes it would be early morning before I went to bed because I needed to know God. I didn't want to know of Him, I needed to know Him for myself. I needed to experience the True and Living God and be strengthened to do what He would ask of me.

One day while I was sitting in the chapel reaching out to God, a group of people came in and invited me to a service they would be holding there later that week. I returned there on the night mentioned and for the life of me I could not tell you what the preacher spoke on that night. I sat there in my chair and it was as if God Almighty was speaking to me and letting me know the love and desire he had for me. I remember sitting in my seat waiting for the call of salvation. I wanted to dedicate my life to the Lord. The desire was so strong that I could not hear anything else as I waited. When the call was made I took all the hurt and pain, which I had accumulated through the years, and I cried myself to freedom as my Heavenly Father embraced me.

The preacher then asked if anyone wanted to be baptized and began to explain to us the promises that accompany baptism. I thought within myself, I'd already been baptized, but everyone else that came up said yes so I said ok too.

They took us back in a room and gave us white robes and explained to us the procedure. When the time came, I watched the people in front on me and all I saw were dry bodies become wet bodies. My heart longed for so much. I needed this to be more than the limitation of man. As I began to walk into the water I realized that God had my undivided attention and He had become first in my life. The Preacher began to speak, I closed my eyes and as I was emerged into the water I saw my death in that water. As I was withdrawn from it, something happened. An unknown presence began to fill me up until I had no more room and when I opened my mouth to speak, a language began to come out from my lips that I had never heard before. I had emptied out all that I thought I needed and wanted. And that which I had not known to desire had been given to me and there were no words to describe the joy and peace, which had been given to me on that day!

This was a very challenging time for me because I was now surrounded by no one. I was in a foreign country and I was alone. The only person I had was the invisible God that my heart now longed to know.

Shortly after that, I began to attend church within an apartment complex in Neu Ulm, West Germany. This church was not what I had been accustomed to, but it was what I needed and so much more. The Pastor had to be hand-picked by God. When you stepped into the room, all you felt was genuine love. The men and the women were on their knees praying. There was such a presence of God there that you did not want to leave. The pastor was just what I needed. I had been over exposed to aggressive and loud men, but this man was humble and very gentle and I needed that in my life. His wife was the lioness and that was great to see and behold also. There was Brother and Sister Day whom I befriended and later became the god mother of their daughter. I would not have imagined that such a place existed; but God always gives us exactly what we need even when we aren't aware of it.

I remember being in the service one day and before I knew it I had shared a moment of my life that once haunted me as a testimony of Grace. Yes, I shared about the rape, pregnancy, and the abortion. Those words had proceeded from my mouth without fear or judgment. The dark hole that had once sucked me so far within itself no longer filled my mind with thoughts of hopelessness. I had peace and not fear concerning my present and future. I had met love face to face and I was experiencing such freedom and life.

I was emailing a friend of mine today between my writing and she said that I possess a courage that she lacked. I replied to her, "I am sorry to disappoint you because that which you describe to be courage is truly a dependency. I am an addict and I will forever need a fix. That which you call courage is what I call my fix." (lol)

I will forever be in need of my Lord and Savior and I am so glad that He is from everlasting to everlasting! My courage is my dependency upon him.

Let me just say this, for reasons God only knows He requires certain acts from certain individuals. Does that make one person better or more special to God versus another person? I think not! It has to do with His purpose and the training needed to prepare us to fulfill our destiny. We all need His amazing grace which was provided through Jesus Christ and we all are asked to present our bodies as a living sacrifice (Romans 12:1), but we all will not and do not hold the same office or position within the body of Christ. We need to search out our place and when we discover it, to do it with all of our might through Christ who strengthens us.

Chapter 18

Forgiveness

"A forgiven life is a forgiving lifestyle"

Where do I begin when I speak about the word forgiveness? This word alone is the recipe of God for freedom. All of us desire to be free from all the lies that have been planted within our soul and whisper to us untrue statements of who we are and where we are headed. I feel so strong in my inner man that forgiveness and faith are the keys to walking in our destiny and fulfilling the mandate of God in our lives. Forgiveness and Faith are the mightiest essentials that we possess within us through love. If you are reading this book, you are longing for a greater understanding of who you are and your purpose as God's child. You are longing to be free from strongholds of traditions, legalism, fear, doubt, imaginations, memories, and from walking carnally or fleshy (which ever word you choose). Some of you reading this book picked it up and did not know why. You were like the people in Paul's day. Acts 17:18a says. *"Then certain philosophers of the Epicureans and the Stoics encounter him and some said; 'what will this babbler say?'"* You have felt that people have been babbling all your life and you are looking and hungry for something that is **tangible, accessible, accredited**, and **sure**.

I used these words because that is what I was looking for, and I found the answer. The answer I found was not given to me by man, nor was it received by me through my perception. In order to receive change, we have to be willing to put away habits! We have to shut them down—to say no to them within our understanding. We have circled this barn too long. The view isn't getting any better. As a matter of fact, it's getting old, distasteful, and boring while creating a yielding for a better view. I pray to the Almighty God of heaven and earth that He would reveal Himself in you and through you. I pray that this book will be an instrument with the flexibility to provide to each reader what they need.

Let's look at our desires. In need of something **tangible**, we as individuals desire to be held and to feel. It is one of our senses that the Creator gave to us whereby we might communicate and fellowship. Tangible: *discernible by the touch or capable of being touched, capable of being treated as fact, capable of being understood or realized.* We need those capabilities in our life. We cannot live productively, nor live the quality of life that was redeemed for us without it. We have heard it before, God is a Spirit and He is. But we need to understand that we are spirit also. The tangibility of God's essence reaches through the walls of our natural being and touches our spiritual being in such a manner that we know without a shadow of doubt that we are at home. We are at peace and rest. When we are touched by this tangible essence, immediately we discern the touch! Immediately it shifts from a thought or perception to a reality!

Immediately it is valued as priceless! There is so much that immediately transpires at the exact moment we are touched that all of our being is overcharged with excitement to the point of tears. The tears flow because of the union. It is the evidence being manifested outwardly that the wall has been broken and that an opportunity has arisen whereby a relationship can be established.

Just as what you are hungry for is tangible, it is also **accessible.** Accessible: *easily approached or entered, easily obtained, easy to get along with.* This is truly the description of our Heavenly Father. We just spoke on the tangibility of His essence. He approaches us first and says hello as He smiles with joy because we have allowed Him permission to get this close. He lets us know through the conversation with the touch that He longs to continue to touch us. He longs to hold us when we feel unlovable and distressed because His touch is easy to be obtained. He listens to the tears as they roll down our cheeks proclaiming our hurt and calamity. He's easy to get along with because He has been waiting so long for this moment—the moment when you allow Him to embrace you with His tangible and accessible being.

As for being **accredited** (*to certify as meeting a prescribed standard*), I must laugh at this. Who could describe God's accreditation? The little that I understand I can share, but I will truly falter. What standard are we looking for? Is it not truth, love, security, stability, and acceptance that we lack in our day-by-day relationships? Well, our Heavenly Father gives us all of this and more on a daily basis. He loves us unconditionally, speaks only the truth to us, has secured us through our inheritance, established us by His commitment, and accepted us in the beloved.

I desperately needed something that was **sure**. As I looked around my life, I felt alone, misunderstood, taken for granted, and imprisoned by my own fears and doubts and shames I was too embarrassed to name. I am certain that I was lost standing in the middle of a busy intersection. People were coming and going all around me but no one stopped to help. The ones at my intersection couldn't help because they were lost too! I was as a blind man without a seeing-eye dog, so I stumbled and fell many times. My many bruises caused me to retrieve to an unknown place, which took me to a deeper place of confusion. There were signs all around me, but I could not read them because I did not know the language. So I became devastated and heartache and misery set in.

Where do you unload such a burden? Sometimes the only place you believe is available is death! It calls to you with a definite end to all your worries and pain. It is definite and it is used as an alternative to the situation at hand, but it is in no way your surety. That which is "sure" is not a quick fix, but it is an immediate change.

Again, I mention the tangible touch, the accessible heart, and reputable standards. All of these sum up to "sure". There is a sure relationship with sure love, respect, and equality.

I mention all of this because at the beginning of this chapter I said the forgiveness and faith are the mightiest essentials in which we possess within us through love. But if we have not experienced love, not the roller coaster ride or the seesaw, but unconditional love, we will not be able to engage those essentials (forgiveness and faith) within our relationships with our family, friends, co-workers, bosses, employees, etc. In order for us to live a lifestyle of forgiving, we have to experience forgiveness. We have to stand before a Holy God and allow Him the ultimate pleasure of washing us. I did not begrudge bathing my children and neither does God, our Father.

When you stand before God naked and your body is tattooed with shame from all of your activities during the course of your life until that day, it is amazing that He does not turn up His nose or say, "you stink!" Oh, He smiles, He laughs, and He rejoices from the depth of His being, my child has come to me! He looks at you with tenderness examining all the markings: rejection, betrayal, lies, rape, disappointment, and so much more or less. It does not matter—He sees it all.

As He examines your hurt and pain, He begins to set the temperature of the water for your cleansing. He goes to the cupboard where all the soap is stored, and considering you in particular, He reaches for the scent that will not only remove your shame, but also heal your pain! He is truly an awesome God! When he places you in that water (only after rechecking the temperature so no more devastation is caused), He embraces you very close so that you know that you are not alone as He immerses you in the water. As you notice the fragrance that is ascending from the water, you are quietly transported in thought to a place of Truth. You see truth and it huddles all around you.

Truth has joined in as the soapsuds in a bubble bath. Fear is no longer present, only a symphony of angels serenading you during your wash. It appears to be faint, but in truth, all of your focus is upon your Father. For the first time, you acknowledge the cloth in His hand that is filled with water and the fragrance. The touch is as the dew of the morning while the water appears to flow under the skin and transcend unto the soul. There is a power, or shall I say a presence, within the water as it begins to purge your very soul.

There are separations taking place within you! All of a sudden, one after another, bubbles begin to emerge from the water and there is captivity within them. Their appearances are different one from another, but they all represent pain, agony, and torment in some way or another. These bubbles were immediately removed from tub and from the vicinity. What an amazing and loving Father! Can you imagine

Him washing your back? Take a moment and close your eyes and when you open them, I will continue the vision of your bath.

He is so amazing! Imagine this: your heavenly Father is a big and mighty God, but at this point in the bath He begins to take on your image. As he does, transference takes place and He is now beside the tub on his knees and his head bowed. Angels begin to descend from the throne room and there is one for each issue upon your back. They line up one behind another and remove the issues from your back. Now they line up behind God who has become a man and one after another your issues are placed upon his back. These issues are in many shapes and forms. One had the appearance of a scorpion and as it was placed upon his back I notice that it stung him and he begun to shake as the poison entered into his body. As I considered the matter, my eyes went to your back, the bruises, knots, and torn tissue that once appeared upon you were no longer there. I had never seen a cleaner, un-blemished back. Won't He make you clean?!

I turn back to notice the angels as another placed what appeared to be a bat upon our savior and it immediately took a hold to his back. I watched as I saw the blood began to be sucked from his body and weakness manifested upon his face. I realized at that moment, you were bathing in the cleansing blood of Jesus! There was distress upon his face, but there was joy upon yours! After each placement, pain and sorrow echoed through his body. I wanted to cry out, make it stop! When I was about to, his hand covered my mouth, and his smile spoke to my heart of his grace and mercy and I knew I had been forgiven.

After the bath, there was a special anointing administered to your body. I watched God in man form now robed in white with oil proceeding out of his hands. As the oil ran out of his hands, he began at the crown of your head to anoint you. It was mesmerizing! With great tenderness and mercy he applied this oil to your body. I remember the anointing being placed upon your lips. As his fingertips began to touch them, something miraculous happened. You turned your head toward heaven and you lifted your hands. For hours, praising proceeded from your mouth. At times your dialect changed, but I still was able to comprehend your words of praise. When his hands reached your heart it begun to dance merrily! I had never ever seen a heart dance; it was a supernatural act of God. It twirled and flipped! It leaped for joy! It actually began to beat with a different rhythm and the sound was soothing. As he finished at the feet, let me just say they were happy. Everything that was under your feet was destroyed! There is no doubt to that.

These are some of the details I imagine concerning our washing and anointing. Focusing again on the main thought of this chapter, forgiveness is a necessary commodity that we cannot live without.

Take in the details of what happens when we are forgiven, which includes us being washed and anointed. How can we go through this process of forgiveness and not share the experience with others?

Forgiveness: (Bible dictionary definition) *An act of God's grace to forget forever and not hold people of faith accountable for the sins they confess; to a lesser degree the gracious human act of not holding wrong acts against a person.* It has both divine and human dimensions. First of all, in the divine relationship it is the gracious act of God by which believers are put into right relationship with God and transferred from spiritual death to spiritual life through the sacrifice of Jesus. It is also, in this divine dimension, the ongoing gift of God without which our lives as Christians would be "out of joint" and full of guilt. In terms of a human dimension, forgiveness is that act and attitude toward those who have wronged us which restores relationships and fellowship.

My definition of forgiveness: Forgiveness is <u>unconditional love</u> in operation.

Love isn't wooden rules, but it governs forgiveness.

I have shared with you a place of helplessness and hopelessness that I experienced in my life. Now I would like to share with you forgiveness. Forgiveness is truly a gift. It can't be placed within any wrapping paper or gift bag because it stands alone in its uniqueness. It is the greatest authority God has given unto men. It is an authority whereby a response from God is caused. It's a gift that continues to give. It isn't a natural plate of food that is given to an individual and eaten. It can't be passed on to another. But this tangible gift that isn't seen, but felt within the depth of one's heart and soul can continue its journey from one heart, mind, and soul to another.

After I went through the ordeal surrounding the abortion, not only was I hurt, I was angry! I was mad because I thought I had a family, a place of safety and security. I was disappointed in the family system. When I needed it to be there for me, my mind said it wasn't. I remember one time being in the bedroom with my mom. I was asking her something that was important to me and she responded in a non-acceptable way and my hand went up to hit her. She didn't see it go up, but it hurt me so bad to even have unresolved issues running through my emotions that these issues would place me in an attack mode towards my mother. I remember turning around in shame, and groaning filled my soul. I knew that I needed help! I needed deliverance and forgiveness for myself and to pass on throughout my household. No one else knew at the time what had happened, but they had become estranged. As I walked out of my mother's room that day, I knew I needed to get away. I have already shared that story; let me now share concerning my visit after I was forgiven.

After God accepted me as His child with all my hurt and issues, I began to seek Him and His righteousness. I remember about a year later coming to visit my mother and having my next to the oldest and baby sister there with me. I did not mention the rape in their presence, but I shared with mom what I had experienced growing up in our household. I shared with her what I felt I had lacked and the outcome from it. She wept and we wept with her.

She began to say how she wasn't taught to communicate with her children. She said that all she knew was to keep us clean, fed, and housed. We all hugged each other and cried. Because I was given the gift of forgiveness, I was able to pass it on to my mother and share it with my sisters and they were able to forgive my mother also. It was such a joyous occasion. There is no greater occasion mentioned in the bible as the occasion of forgiveness. Luke 15:7 says, "*I say unto you, that likewise joy shall be in heaven over one sinner that repents, more than over ninety and nine just persons which need no repentance*". It says that <u>more joy shall be in heaven</u> over one sinner that repents than ninety-nine just persons. Did you see that? More! So there is rejoicing for the righteous, but there is a <u>greater rejoicing</u> for the repentant sinner. Why? Because of the free gift. If the gift of forgiveness was not available, why would there be a need for repentance?

Repentance says, "I am willing and ready for change concerning my ways and actions." While forgiveness says, "I am ready to erase all that you have done until now and believe your willingness to change; but if you are unable, all is still forgiven."

Before this verse, Jesus speaks about a shepherd who has lost a sheep and after finding it, he calls his friends and celebrates. Forgiveness causes our lost to be found! If the shepherd's attitude was nasty and he didn't care for his position or the lost, he would not have gone looking for the sheep. He would have accepted his lost! But the sheep was important to him! Are not your family and friends important?

The lost sheep wasn't with the other sheep, but it did not know that it was lost—it only knew that it was alone. When that shepherd found it, it understood that it belonged. My mom belonged in my heart. She was a part of my life. She had been separated from me by an act, but forgiveness restored her proper place in my heart. Take the time to restore those individuals in your heart.

Chapter 19

God Wants to Anoint You!

*The Lord is my shepherd. I shall not want. ²He maketh
me to lie down in green pastures: He leadeth me beside
still waters. ³He restoreth my soul; He leadeth me in the
paths of righteousness for His name's sake. ⁴Yea, though
I walk through the valley of the shadow of death, I will
fear no evil: for thou art with me; thy rod and thy staff
they comfort me. ⁵Thou preparest a table before me in
the presence of mine enemies; thou anointest my head
with oil; my cup runneth over. ⁶Surely goodness and
mercy shall follow me all the days of my life; and I will
dwell in the house of the Lord forever.*

Psalm 23

For many reasons, I know at times we feel that we have committed
an unpardonable sin. Sometimes it is because of the repetition of the
sin, because we overlooked the warnings that were before us, (those
big neon lights blinking one foot in front of us), or various other
reasons. We feel that we will never succeed, nor live a sanctified life.
We can and we must! We must to fulfill who we are in Christ Jesus.
We must to claim our seat at the table! **The table of anointing**.
This is a very special place, and during our journey we must learn
forgiveness.

The main scriptures I am looking at are Psalms 23:5-6.

⁵Thou preparest a table before me in the presence of mine enemies; thou anointest my head with oil; my cup runneth over. ⁶Surely goodness and mercy shall follow me all the days of my life; and I will dwell in the house of the Lord forever.

In verse 1 He becomes our shepherd because he sought us out when we were lost. And He brings all the provision that His sheep will ever need.

In verse 2 He allows us to lie down without feeling threatened in the best pasture. Green pasture, not brown or dried up pasture. Now when He found us, we were wandering around and stressed out. He wants to take us to our destiny, but the perfect elements are needed throughout the journey. The green pastures are great! But we need to wash it down! We can become thirsty on the journey and the good shepherd knows that he must meet the need, or we **will** wander off looking to quench our thirst on our own. He also understands that we are more likely to drink in the still waters. If the waters are turbulent, we could die of thirst because we would be too afraid to drink! One of the biggest issues Moses had to deal with was leading a "thirsty bunch" of people that murmured and complained <u>in part</u> because there was not water available for them at any given point on the journey. I am in no way justifying their action, just trying to show you the provision of the Lord. At anytime on the journey, we can bend over, use our own hand/hands and take a drink of "still water". That's refreshing even at the thought!

In verse 3 He gave back to us the most sacred thing we once possessed, our soul. Our ability to think outside the leadership of darkness; to experience and feel love deeper than we had ever known; to remember who God is, and to imagine the impossible! And since He knows the territory (because He has already journeyed through it), He offers Himself as our guide. He knows that any and every path will not accomplish the preparation work that is needed. So He leads us through proven ground concerning the success of His prior journey alone.

I believe that it is so important that even as Jesus had to **forgive** while He hung on that cross, so do we. As He hung there, the paths of righteousness were being paved. As He looked around and beheld all the people who mocked, spat, beat, drove nails through His hands and feet, and shouted "away with man," He laid the last stone when He looked up and said, "Father, forgive them, they know not what they do." After He withdrew all their debts, He said it is finished. Three days and nights later, He rose with all power and might because un-forgiveness is judgment (we assume to know better). Christ accepted His role as man, and as man He knew that He had to forgive us so that we might have our rightful place in the Father's heart.

I would like to take a moment to share a dream I had about many of the saints of God. I became aware of a place in my dream; it looked as if it was a cave. As I began to walk and look around, I noticed the ground to be of sand. I also noticed that the path went in only one direction. I did not see any intersection that would cause a traveler to have to decide which way to go. The path was narrow, but it continued to go forward as I moved forward. I am sure I could have turned back if I wanted, but it never came to my mind to do such a thing.

As I found myself going deeper into this place, I also noticed that I was walled in on both sides, and again, the path was narrow. At last I saw an entry, but was not aware that it was such. However, I could not avoid where the path was taking me. The entry wasn't very wide either. As a matter of fact, I had to stoop down to take a look. When I did . . . it was amazing! I saw footprints first. Then I saw feet of the individuals who had made the prints. They were in front of me within the area I was gazing upon. They were running and it appeared that they were playing and having fun. I decided to go in. When I stepped into this place I knew where I was . . . I was in the heart of God!

I saw and I heard the beat of His heart. Who would have known and believed such a thing? I stood there very quiet and stood as I beheld the heart of my God. Words cannot and will not do this experience justice. Jesus forgave so that I could find my way back to the heart of God. I can still remember it and see the feet and the children running. I can still hear the joy that was there all around me. Even now, tears swell in my eyes as I recall this experience. Are you not willing to forgive so that someone, and even yourself, might find the way back to the heart of God? The rhythm and the sounds I heard are still in my ears. It is my heart's desire to fulfill His desire for me.

In verse 4 we have become dependent, reliant, safe, secure and aware of His works. We open our mouth to speak and our words are of faith, hope and confidence! We speak of that we know and not of what someone has mentioned in passing. We are presently traveling on a journey that appears to be dangerous, but our words are bold and steadfast—we will not back down! We have embraced our shepherd, friend, and lover. We have learned to count on Him.

What a friend we have in Jesus!

Now let's look at the main scripture that concludes the matter. God desires to anoint you; but before this can happen, all of these things that I mention in Psalms 23 must take place.

Thou preparest a table before me in the presence of mine enemies; thou anointest my head with oil; my cup runneth over.

Are you willing to give this all up because you prefer to harness un-forgiveness in your heart?

He made the table ready in advance for a particular purpose, event and occasion. The **purpose** would be the hour that you truly understood who you were in the beloved. The **event** would be happening during your journey through the valley of the shadow of death. The **occasion** would be your proper anointing before all of your enemies to be used for the kingdom.

God prepares the table before you; but as you stand at a distance, what He is preparing may not look that delicious at first. Nevertheless, preparation is taking place. You may not be able to see or smell what is being placed on the table, but it is all being prepared for your honor—**right here and right now if you have made it to this place and are proclaiming your protection by His rod and staff.** There is a preparation taking place on your behalf. God is preparing though the table may not be finished right at this moment. Get ready!

The bible dictionary declares that a table is an article of furniture used for rituals, eating and money exchanging. David offered places at his table to those to whom he felt indebted. Do you realize that as a child of God, God is indebted to you as your Father? I Timothy 5:8 says, *"But if any provide not for his own; and especially for those of his own house, he hath denied the faith and is worse than an infidel."*

I say this because God does not call us to a different standard, but the same. He says to *"be yet Holy for I am Holy"* I Peter 1:16.

In a symbolic way, the word "table" is sometimes used to describe abundant provision.

Presence of enemies: you have reached a place in your life and in your relationship with God the Father and you know that God has your back. You do not have to be concerned about what the enemy is doing. He's looking at what you are doing! And he's watching what is being done to you! It's all about what God has placed before you now! **There is a word spoken concerning you and no evil can come near your dwelling!**

Anointed my head: *God wants to anoint you!* Anoint is to authorize, or set apart, a person for a particular work or service (Isa. 61:1). The anointed person belongs to God in a special sense. The phrases 'the Lord's anointed', 'God's anointed', 'my anointed', 'your anointed', or 'His anointed' are used of Saul, David and Solomon. Anointing in the New Testament also refers to the anointing of the Holy Ghost, which brings understanding. The Holy Ghost anoints a person's heart and mind with the love and truth of God.

Cup: no dinner party is a success without a cup of something. The cup of blessings (I Cor. 10:16) is what we are served by our cupbearer (Jesus). He has already tasted of the cup and informed us that it is safe. Scripture says, "My cup runneth over." There are abundant blessings such as: light from darkness, understanding, wisdom, healing, comfort, deliverance, prosperity, no lack, healthy relationship with God and man, etc.

Surely: There is a conclusion to this matter. If I am here, I am here! Here I will remain!

Chapter 20

Everyone Needs Forgiveness

Forgiveness is God's Recipe for freedom

The basic facts of the Bible are God's creative power and holiness; human rebellion, and the efforts of our merciful God to bring us back to an intended relationship of son-ship and fellowship. The need of forgiveness is first seen in the third chapter of Genesis, as Adam and Eve willfully disobeyed God, choosing rather to satisfy their own self will. The results were guilt (Gen. 3:8, 10), separation from God, loss of fellowship (Gen. 3:8, 23-24), and a life of hardships, anxiety, and death (Gen. 3:16-24).

God has forgiven you!

Romans 3:22-25 states:

> *²²Even the righteousness of God which is by faith of Jesus Christ unto all and upon all them that believe: for there is no difference: ²³For all have sinned and come short of the glory of Glory of God; ²⁴Being justified freely by His grace through the redemption that is in Christ Jesus. ²⁵Whom God hath set forth to be a propitiation through faith in his blood, to declare his righteousness for the remission of sins that are past, through the forbearance of God.*

I think one of the hardest things for us to do is to forgive ourselves. We let go of the ego and emotional ties which have offended us through others and we release forgiveness to that person, but somehow we still kick ourselves in the butt concerning our part in the matter. I will drop to my knees quickly when someone has hurt me to release them before the throne of grace. But I would tear myself up, call myself names, and just let myself have it when I failed in a battle. Unconsciously I must have believed that I was not worthy of forgiveness. I held myself to a different standard. I guess I thought God's standards were beneath me; or I had so much pride that I spoke the words to myself, "you know better than that;" as if I were infallible, perfect Rene'. That isn't reality! Reality is, I am the righteousness of God through Christ Jesus, but my sanctification is a process. The longevity of the process depends upon my willingness to give myself to the word, spirit, and to others.

My main reason for writing this book was to encourage others through their transitioning from glory to glory to keep the faith. I know that God still does all that He did in Jesus' day. He is just hoping for a generation who will hold Him accountable. But we can't and won't if we will not forgive ourselves. We will never be worthy in the carnal person who loves darkness because it was born in darkness. Darkness produced our natural man! That is why Jesus said, "You must be born again." Once you have taken the step of salvation, you are born again and like Patti Labelle sings, "I have a new attitude."

The first thing on your list should be:

#1 Accept your forgiveness √

If we do not accept amazing grace for our own selves, how are we made whole? Aren't you tired of making excuses for why you haven't gotten out there and fulfilled your dreams? The time is now! Settle it in your heart. I'm forgiven!

This book "Being found in Him" was the name the Lord gave to me years ago when He placed it upon my heart to write it. This is the foundation scripture found on the cover page:

Philippians 3:9-10

> *⁹And **being found in him**, not having mine own righteousness which is the law, but that which is through the faith of Christ, the righteousness which is of God by faith. ¹⁰That I may know him, and the power of his resurrection, and the fellowship of his sufferings, being made conformable unto his death; If by any means I might attain unto the resurrection of the dead.*

Being found in him is only a fraction of my story; and it is also my life and meaning. This scripture says, "Not having mine own righteousness." If the miracles I received depended upon my acts and works, this book would not have been written. For that I am eternally grateful. This story is about each and every one of us. It may be shared through my experiences, but in some way on your journeys you have encountered loss, betrayal, fear, temptation, and much more.

The question is, what do we do when these storms arise? Be found "not having your own righteousness." Have that which is given through the faith of Christ. I shared with you how I came home from the hospital and bowed at the side of my bed and prayed for my ex-husband. From the sincerity of my heart I asked God if when he stands before Him that his sin against me (which was truly against God only as the psalmist said in Psalms 51:4a; against thee, thee only, have I sinned and done this evil in thy sight) might be forgiven because I forgive him as Christ forgave me. Lord God, forgive this man because he knows not what he does.

All of us who have been forgiven need to adapt this concept of truth. Forgive them because they know not what they do. You think differently; if they really understood the consequences of their actions, I do not believe that their actions would be such. The bottom line though, Jesus is our example; we have to forgive to be His disciples. Therefore,

Let go of:

    A. <u>Guilt:</u> we try to justify our feelings, but we can't by the word of God.

    B. <u>Separation:</u> trying to avoid the other person which results in loss of fellowship. Sometimes we might not be able to heal the relationship, but it will be in God's hand and in His time.

    C. <u>Life of hardships:</u> two can do labor easier than one (Ecclesiastes 2:9).

    D. <u>Anxiety:</u> from being alone, feeling alone, and as if you don't belong. You have a place at the table and there are others there with you in the Kingdom of our Father.

These produce stress factors that give birth to illness and diseases, which end in premature death. That isn't your destiny!

"That I may know Him and the power of His resurrection and the fellowship of His sufferings being made conformable unto His death."

This scripture above says that if we walk in the righteousness of Christ (forgiveness), we are setting ourselves up to **know** Him and the **manifestation of the power** of his resurrection. **Only** because I took all the word of God (that I understood) and meditated upon it day and night, was I victorious in my life. Since I can remember, forgiveness has been a priority to me. The scripture says in Matthew 5:7, *"Blessed are the merciful, they shall attain mercy."* You do not know when you will need mercy in your life, so store it up now!

The second thing on your list should be:

#2 Forgive yourself √

The third thing on your list should be:

#3 Forgive others √

This is the will of God concerning you!

The conclusion of the matter is found in the following scriptures:

Matthew 6:12—*And forgive us our debt, as we forgive our debtors (what is owed)*

Matthew 6:14—*For if ye forgive men their trespasses, your heavenly Father will also forgive you* (God uses you to manifest His righteousness. You want to be used, let Him use you to forgive . . . that's ministry!)

Matthew 18:21-35

> *[21] Then came Peter to him and said, Lord how oft shall my brother sin against me. And I forgive him? Till seven times? [22] Jesus saith unto him, I say not unto thee, until seven times: but until seventy times seven. [23] Therefore, is the kingdom of heaven likened unto a certain king, which would take account of his servants. [24] And when he had begun to reckon, one was brought unto him, which owed him ten thousand talents. [25] But foreasmuch as he had not to pay, his lord commanded him to be sold, and his wife, and children, and all that he had, and payment to be made. [26] The servant therefore fell down, and worshipped him, saying, Lord, have patience with me, and I will pay thee all. [27] Then the lord of that servant was moved with compassion, and loosed him, and forgave him the debt.*
>
> *[28] But the same servant went out, and found one of his fellowservants, which owed him an hundred pence: and he laid hands on him, and took him by the throat, saying, Pay me that thou owest. [29] And his fellowservant fell down at his feet, and besought him, saying, Have patience with me, and I will pay thee all. [30] And he would not: but went and cast him into prison, till he should pay the debt. [31] So*

when his fellowservants saw what was done, they were very sorry, and came and told unto their Lord all that was done. [32]Then his lord, after that he had called him, said unto him, O thou wicked servant, I forgave thee all that debt, because thou desiredst me: [33]Shouldest not thou also have had compassion on the fellowservant, even as I had pity on thee? [34]And his lord was wroth, and delivered him to the tormentors, till he should pay all that was due unto him. [35]So likewise shall my heavenly Father do also unto you, if ye from your hearts forgive not every ne his brother their trespasses.

The key concepts from this scripture I want to emphasize are as follows"

A. Verse 25; remember that unforgiveness affects the whole family
B. Verse 30; cast him into prison, till he should pay the debt (stop thinking like the world). Spiritual beings forgive because they understand the warfare in the flesh*!*
C. Verse 35; so likewise shall my heavenly Father do also unto you, if ye *from your hearts* forgive not everyone his brother/sister their **trespasses.** When someone trespasses against you, they knew they shouldn't, but did it anyway. They saw the signs to stay back, but crossed the fence anyhow and touched you where they shouldn't have and took what they should not have.

Forgiveness is God's Recipe for Freedom

Set the atmosphere:

1. Make your mind an altar and prepare to lay all unforgiveness there.
2. Play a song (even in your head). Set a tone of worship (forgiveness is worship).
3. Keep the lights down low—don't over-think it (and begin to judge again).

4. Place the person down on your forgiveness/mercy seat and release them . . . and set your heart, emotions, mind, and will free!

Sometimes you need to set the atmosphere to forgive yourself also:

1. See yourself (with all your imperfections—remember all your failures, inabilities, mistakes, regrets, etc. See yourself naked and don't move.) **Turn the lights high!**
2. Wash yourself (II Cor. 5:17; *Therefore if any man be in Christ, he is a new creature: old things are passed away; behold all things are become new*).
3. Now sing a new song: I am free . . . I've been redeemed by the Blood of the Lamb! (Encourage yourself in the Lord).
4. Love yourself unconditionally (while looking in God's mirror) Cor. 3:18 *But we all, with open face beholding as in a glass the glory of the Lord, are changed into the same image from glory to glory, even as by the Spirit of the Lord.*
5. Take a seat on your forgiveness/mercy seat and release yourself . . . let the tears fall, let the cleanser, healer, and deliverer in so that His work might be perfected in you.
6. Forgive yourself for who you aren't and who you were, for not praying, lack of devotion toward God, disobedience, your past, present, dishonoring your parents, grandparents, abusing your children, adultery, fornicating, judging, instigating, justifying yourself, causing hurt to others, mistakes, stupidity, having sex out of wedlock, abortion, drugs, alcohol, homosexuality, murder, stealing, cheating, lying, betrayal, what you can no longer do, etc . . .
7. Know that you are accepted in the beloved! *Being found in Him!*

Chapter 21

Faith . . .

. . . Now Faith is the substance of things hoped for; the evidence of things unseen.

Hebrews 11:1

I have mentioned faith and forgiveness a couple of times in this book, but I have not spoken about faith in the same amount of detail as I have about forgiveness. So give me a little more of your time and let's explore faith for a while.

We have a major scripture concerning faith that instructs us that without it, there is no way that we can please God.

Hebrews 11: 5-6

> *⁵By faith Enoch was translated that he should not see death and was not found because God had translated him: for before his translation he had this testimony, that he pleased God.*
>
> *⁶But without faith it is impossible to please him. For He that cometh to God must believe that He is, and that he is a rewarder of them that diligently seek Him.*

Look at the testimony of Enoch! Faith is a very powerful ally to have. Death did not even come his way. He knew family members that had passed on, but death never introduced itself to Enoch because God was so pleased with their relationship He would not allow death. Can you imagine exercising your faith in such a manner that it causes God to do the extraordinary? He did it for Enoch, why would He not do it for you? What did Enoch do that others were not doing in his day? Genesis 5:22-24 says,

> *22 And Enoch walked with God after he begat Methuselah three hundred years and begat sons and daughters; 23 and all the days of Enoch were three hundred sixty and five years: 24 And Enoch walked with God: and he was not: for God took him.*

Enoch could have gotten distracted with all of his sons and daughters and made their situations and circumstances priority and not his relationship with God. Instead, he maintained his relationship with his wife, which is evident because after he began his walk with God he has sons and daughters. God didn't just take Enoch and leave his house in disarray; He had Methuselah ready to take up his inheritance and also blessed him with long life that surpassed any other. I believe that the faith that Enoch manifested toward God through his commitment and fellowship extended the life of his first son. Faith has a powerhouse of benefits!

On the other hand, without it you cannot please God. That's saying a lot! In the natural, how do we as children please our parents? We do so by obeying their instructions and by living our lives accordingly. But you can't live your life according to God's instructions if you do not have faith in Him. That is why the next part of the scripture says *"he that cometh to God must believe that he is."* Somewhere between birth and your first steps you begin to say "da da" and your parents get excited and say she/he called you daddy. And you believe that he is. Somewhere in Enoch's walk he knew that God was God so he stayed close by Him and refused to settle for anything less and God translated him.

Faith is a precious substance that we as children of God can't afford not to have. We need faith to forgive.

Luke 17:3-5

³Take heed to yourselves: if thy brother trespass against thee, rebuke him; and if he repent, forgive him.
⁴And if he trespass against thee seven times in a day and seven times in a day, turn again to thee saying, I repent, thou shall forgive him.
⁵And the Apostles said unto the Lord, increase our faith.

Jesus goes on in verse 6 and gives them a great example using the sycamore tree to show the power and results of faith. In other words, faith is an enabler. Faith enables you to do the impossible with supernatural results! Then from verses 7-9 he gives a word of thought saying *"when you have done all those things which are commanded you, say, we are unprofitable servants; we have done that which was our duty to do."* Enoch thought it to be his duty to walk with the Lord and he took pride and pleasure in his relationship.

Faith is generated by love and love creates forgiveness. Love and forgiveness are joined, you can't truly love and not forgive, nor can you forgive someone with hatred. Let's have faith and see the supernatural works of God in our lives during impossible situations.

Chapter 22

Will you let Him Ride?

I remember when I received a word from God telling me to be like a racehorse. He actually said, "I need you to be like a racehorse with blinders on."

He was letting me know that I was about to travel upon uncharted territory and it would be difficult. All that I was accustomed to seeing, feeling, smelling, tasting, and hearing was about to change greatly. The enemy had compromised my path. He had set up roadblocks by planting weapons of destruction throughout my path. The only way I was going to survive and make it through this valley was to have faith in His leadership.

He asked me not to use my sight, but to depend on Him to lead me across this wasteland. Proverbs 3:5 says, "*Trust the Lord with all thine heart; and lean not unto thine own understanding. In all thy ways acknowledge Him, and He shall direct thy paths.*" This journey would begin to teach me the strength and the amazing works of God on a new level.

The first word says, "trust." Trust is a characteristic of faith. It is impossible for you to have faith in someone and not have trust. These two powerful words are joined together at the heart. God was asking me to allow my faith to be activated for use. He was saying, "Rene', you have faith, show me your faith in action". In the epistle, **James** says the same thing. 2:18 "*Yes, a man may say, thou has faith and I have works; show me your faith without works and I will show you my faith by my works.*

God wanted my faith to begin to create works on a new level. In order for me to do that, I had to be willing to depend upon His leadership over very rough and life threatening terrain.

I could feel the road under my feet—it was harsh, very bumpy and filled with thorns. The sounds that I heard was not friendly voices, instead they were sounds that haunt you in the night. Those sounds that make you turn in all directions looking for the source. God did not want me to be distracted by the voice nor by its words.

How many of you have ever allowed someone to blindfold you? I remember being blind folded to play pin-the-tail-on-the-donkey. You begin by seeing the donkey, next you are blindfolded, and then you are spun around. Afterwards you must depend upon your memories of your surroundings to direct you to that donkey.

God doesn't want you to depend upon your memories. He does not want you to depend upon your touch. He does not want you to depend "at all" upon your reasoning or thoughts. He wants you to depend upon Him.

When I have played the game pin-the-tail-on-the-donkey, sometimes I did well, but other times my tail was nowhere near the donkey's rear. I thought it was near the rear when I pinned the tail, but when the blindfold was removed, the results were not what I had hoped.

God wants our results to always be exceeding abundantly above all that we ask or think. This is what Ephesians 3:20 says!

Allow God to ride you through the darkest times in your life. Don't buck! Settle down and take in the comfort and confidence of your rider. Release yourself from all worry and stress and let the peace of the one that holds your reins (the leather strap that attaches to the bit in the month) lead you to your destiny.

He is riding me now,

Rene' Gloria Hood

Lord I pray that this book will accomplish all that you have sent it out to do for your glory and for your people. In Jesus' Name, Amen.

Appendices

Appendix A is filled with medical statements and lab results to confirm my testimony of God's amazing grace and healing power that is accessible to each one of us.

Appendix B is a thesis I wrote for a Philosophy class when I'd gone back to school. I would like to share this thesis with you in hope of it being a blessing to you.

Appendix A

Medical Reports

I will offer a little narrative to explain the documents you are reading.

I do hope that these truths will rekindle your faith, cause you to believe and strengthen your expectations in the Lord.

Pages 1-4:

These reports describe the Doctor's assessment and comments. They mention Collagen Vascular Disease, Lupus, Anemia and Iron Deficiency, Abdominal pain, Nausea, Vomiting, Fever, Spontaneous Bacterial Peritonitis, deterioration, and a few other things.

These conditions are harsh and the pain affects the emotional person as much as the physical being, but God is able to conquer it all when we stay focused and place our trust in him. I'm no super woman, but the word of God is sure and faithful, you can rest in it.

MRN: 3541531
ANDERSON, RENE
07/28/1959
NAME: 34..777236

①

ZCZC

**SCOTT AND WHITE
ADMISSION HISTORY AND PHYSICAL**

DATE:
CHIEF COMPLAINT
PRESENT ILLNESS
(As appropriate, p
emotional, behavi
social name)
PAST MEDICAL HI
Allergies
Medications
(Children & Adol
developmental s
education needs
daily activities
immunization st
PSYCHOSOCIAL
PERSONAL HIST
FAMILY HISTORY

REVIEW OF SYS
a. General:
b. Skin:
c. Head:
d. Eyes:
e. Ears:
f. Nose:
g. Mouth &
h. Respirato
i. Neurolog
j. Musculos

k. Cardiova
l. Gastroint
m. Urinary:
n. Genitore
o. Endocrin
p. Hematol
q. Psycho

PHYSICAL EX
1. General
2. Vital Sig
3. Skin:
4. Head:
5. Eyes:
6. Ears:
7. Nose &
8. Mouth:
9. Throat
10. Neck:
11. Thorax
12. Breast
13. Lungs:
14. Heart
15. Abdon
16. Genit
17. Vagina
18. Rectal
19. Musc
20. Lymp
21. Bloos
22. Neur
IMPRESSIC
TREATMEN

PATIENT NAME: ANDERSON, RENE***

DATE: 07/27/98   STC-3   MRN: 3541531

The patient is a 39-year-old black female referred by Dr.
in Brownwood for evaluation of nephrotic syndrome in the
setting of apparent collagen vascular disease, but now admitted
because of fever, chills, and increasing abdominal pain suggesting
bacterial peritonitis.

The patient is exceedingly complex. She has never been seen in the
Scott and White system before. She was apparently in her usual state
of health until about 1-1/2 years ago, that is around the first part
of 1997. She began having some arthralgias and aching hands at
night. This continued off and on. She really went almost a full
year longer before she ever saw a physician for these arthralgias.
She denied any other major trouble at that time. She eventually went
to see a physician in February 1998 and apparently got to Dr.
At that time, evaluation there showed leukopenia, anemia (which was
thought to be iron deficient), positive ANA at 1:640, negative DNA,
negative anti-Sm, negative RNP, and a positive SS-A and SS-B.
Subsequent to that, she has really kind of had a slow deteriorating
process with intermittent problems. She has had a lot of trouble in
her right shoulder with occasional intermittent flares in her right
knee of frank arthritis. She denies any skin problems. She had a
rash on her face several weeks ago that was thought to be scleredema
or an allergic reaction with swelling up around her eyes. She is on
no other major medications. In the past several weeks she has been
on Plaquenil. She was on a short course of steroids until about
July 4, lasting about six to 10 days apparently. She tapered because
of this scleral swelling and facial swelling.

In the last two months, she has had increased evidence of ascites,
mild peripheral edema, increasing problems severely in the right
shoulder when she tries to breath, increasing dyspnea and shortness
of breath with lying down, peripheral edema, swallowing difficulties,
nosebleeds, and just otherwise progressively getting worse.

She has seen Dr.   recently. Some laboratory studies done show a
normal BUN of 8 and creatinine of 0.9. Albumin is 2.6, SGOT is
slightly elevated at 37, white count is 2200 with 34 polys,
hemoglobin is 10.8, sedimentation rate is 48, and marked proteinuria
is noted. A 24-hour urine for creatinine and protein, ANA profile,
C3, and C4 were apparently drawn last week, but I do not have the
results of any of that yet. Dr.   on discussion with him today,
will be faxing that information to us as soon as it becomes
available.

SCOTT & WHITE
HISTORY AND PHYSICAL EXAMINATION

LY
MRN: 3541531
NAME: EYCLEPSON, PEVE
00 077.671959
C802 343 772320

②

He saw her three days ago and she clearly was doing poorly. He
called and arranged for her to come down here to be evaluated. In
the interim, however, the patient has developed increasing problems
with nausea and vomiting the last three days with chills and fever,
the exact degree of fever is unclear. Increasing abdominal pain in
the bilateral lower quadrant and into the back. She had a pelvic
exam last week that was unremarkable. Pap smear was done with no
other apparent abnormalities then. She has had no discharge, GU, or
gynecologic symptomatology. Now she just says she feels so miserable
that when she was riding down here today, when they hit a bump or
turned a curve, her stomach would shake a little and she would have
marked discomfort. She has had some degree of loose stools as well.

She has had cough and shortness of breath, but no major active sinus
trouble more than she usually has. She has had no skin lesions. She
has been taking no steroids or immunosuppressive agents recently.

MEDICAL HISTORY: Except as above is unremarkable.

SURGICAL HISTORY: She had a tubal pregnancy and had surgery with
one tube removed in 1990. No other surgery.

SOCIAL HISTORY: She is a nonsmoker, nondrinker. She lives with
her husband and two children, a daughter age 18 and a son age 14.
She is a dental assistant. Her husband works for the state school as
a supervisor. The patient was born and raised in the Washington D.C.
area.

ALLERGIES: No drug allergies.

MEDICATIONS:
1.   Furosemide 80 mg 1 to 2 q.d., 1 yesterday and none today.
2.   Plaquenil in the past.
3.   Ambien in the past.
4.   Prednisone three weeks ago.
5.   Pepcid in the past.
6.   Zyrtec in the past.

FAMILY HISTORY: Father is alive and well at 66. Mother is 62
with hypertension and diabetes. One brother and four sisters. One
sister, age 35, has scleroderma with previous drug use. One sister,
age 40, has hypertension and also was involved in drugs in the past.

REVIEW OF SYSTEMS: No major headaches except when she coughs a lot
she gets a pounding headache. She has had no photophobia, but she
has the eye findings as noted previously with scleredema and

puffiness around the face. She has had swallowing difficulties
recently suggestive of the type she gets with scleroderma. She has
had dry eyes and a dry mouth. She has had marked shortness of
breath, PND, and orthopnea. She was told on an x-ray recently that
she might have had some fluid. She has never had any heart disease,
but she has marked tachycardia today. She has been having nausea and
vomiting for three days. She has had some diarrhea off and on. She
has lost weight from fluid pills, but she does not really think her
weight has changed much. GYN-wise, she had heavy menses for a while.
In the last few months they have been relatively heavy, but only two
or three days rather than heavy for multiple longstanding bleeding
for weeks. She has hematologic problems shown to be leukopenic and
anemic with iron deficiency by bone marrow biopsy three or four
months ago. Joint-wise, she has really been less active recently
than usual. The right knee is better. The hands are better when the
edema is reduced with the diuretics in the last 10 days. Actually,
that part has been better. She has had tenderness of the thyroid
area recently in the last few days. No other skin or rash problems
on review of systems.

PHYSICAL EXAMINATION:

General: Well-developed, well-nourished, acutely
ill-appearing black female.

Vitals: Blood pressure is 116/90 with a pulse of 112
lying and 102/80 with a pulse of about 130
standing. Temperature is 100.3 orally. She
feels quite warm.

HEENT: Fundi are benign. Oropharynx is normal.
No cervical adenopathy. There is fairly

Neck: substantial tenderness right over the thyroid.
No cervical adenopathy.

Lymphatic: No axillary adenopathy.

Lungs: Dullness at the bases. A few crackles.

Heart: Regular rhythm. S4. No S3 or rub. Somewhat
tachycardic. Careful examination does not show a
rub.

Abdomen: Tenderness with rebound tenderness diffusely.
Fluid wave of ascites. No localizing mass.
Spleen is not palpated.

Rectal: Not done. Normal last week.

Pelvic: Not done. Normal last week.

Extremities: No cyanosis or clubbing. No substantial ankle
edema. Ankle pulses, carotid and femoral without
bruits.

Rheumatologic: No active inflammatory joint changes now with
some minimal tenderness over some of the joints,
but no objective findings.

Neurologic: Nonfocal.

Dermatologic: No major lesions. No hair loss.

LABORATORY:
Urinalysis shows 2 to 3+ protein, a few white
cell casts, and hyaline casts. No red cell casts. Otherwise benign
sediment. Certainly no evidence of infection as far as bacteria
seen.

DATE:
CHIEF COMPLAI
PRESENT ILLNE
(As appropriate,
emotional, beh
social status)
PAST MEDICAL
Allergies
Medications
(Children & Adu
developmental
education neces
daily activities
immunization s
PSYCHOSOCIAL
PERSONAL HIST
FAMILY HISTO!

REVIEW OF SYS
a. General
b. Skin
c. Head:
d. Eyes:
e. Ears:
f. Nose:
g. Mouth &'
h. Respirato
i. Neurolog
j. Musculos!

k. Cardiovas
l. Gastroint
m. Urinary
n. Genitoreg
o. Endocrin
p. Hematolo
q. Psycholog

PHYSICAL EXA
1. General S
2. Vital Signs
3. Skin:
4. Head:
5. Eyes:
6. Ears:
7. Nose & S
8. Mouth:
9. Throat:
10. Neck
11. Thorax, I
12. Breasts:
13. Lungs:
14. Heart:
15. Abdome
16. Genitour
17. Vaginal:
18. Rectal:
19. Musculo
20. Lymphat
21. Blood V
22. Neurolo
IMPRESSION/
TREATMENT I

MR Form
1/92

3541531
MRN:
ENDERS R.RENE
DOB 07/04/1959
ACCT 34 772236
NAME:

Ⓐ

ASSESSMENT:

1. Collagen vascular disease that remains very active, probably both serologically and clinically.
2. Nephrotic syndrome, most likely "idiopathic" type glomerulonephritis, but certainly may be related to a lupus type picture with complements and multiple deposits, etc.
3. Abdominal pain, nausea, vomiting, and fever suggestive of spontaneous bacterial peritonitis or some other significant intra-abdominal pathology.
4. Anemia, both iron deficient and otherwise.

She has deteriorated clearly the last several days with fever, chills, and abdominal pain. This suggests significant intra-abdominal pathology. That needs to be assessed in the hospital and evaluated with a paracentesis for cultures and probable CAT scan evaluation if we can get that settled somewhere along the line fairly soon. She probably needs a kidney biopsy for better delineation of the degree of histologic involvement and the nature of the immune deposits, both by immunofluorescence, etc., to see whether she has an "idiopathic" form of glomerulonephritis or a classic typical lupus nephritis. Those would help guide the long-term immunotherapy.

I have talked to her again about a kidney biopsy, and she is very reluctant since she had the problems with previous bone marrow. I also talked to her about a paracentesis, which I think she needs urgently today. I have also talked to her about the long-term steroids, which she does not like, and the short courses of Imuran and prednisone in place of Imuran and Cytoxan depending on the nature of the kidney biopsy and other serologic studies.

She will be admitted on the hospital service under the care of Dr.   I talked to her primary care physician through Blue Cross/Blue Shield, Dr.   , who approved this admission here. I will keep him informed and work with him on a regular basis during her hospitalization and discharge, and then go from there. I reviewed all this in detail with the patient, the daughter who came with her, Dr.   (the referring physician), and Dr.   (the receiving hospital physician).

MD

M.D./fbm
dd: 07/27/98   dt: 07/27/98
JOB #: 235062

cc: Dr.

Page 5:

This report shows the elevated right lung that felt as if I had a huge block stuck in my right side. I felt pressure against my rib (as if the block was trying to get out) causing me to have shortness of breath.

Scott & White Radiology

RADIOLOGY IMAGING CONSULTATION

Page 1 of 1

Name: RENE ANDERSON   Ord. Dr.: CHARLES J. FOULKS, M.D.
MRN#: 3541531   Desk/Room: 3STC
DOB: 07/04/59   Age: Sex: F
Address:
City: State: Zip:

Procedure Requested: CHEST2VIEWS / CHESTXRAYSPECIALVIEWSLATAE

Date of Study: 07/28/98   Time of Study:
Reason/History: FUONBILATERALINFILTRA

RENE ANDERSON 3541531
PA AND LATERAL CHEST X-RAY: Cardiac silhouette and pulmonary vasculature
are within normal limits. The right hemidiaphragm is elevated. A left
pleural effusion is present. Lung fields are otherwise clear of acute
infiltrate.
LEFT LATERAL DECUBITUS X-RAY: The right hemidiaphragm remains elevated.
The left pleural effusion is seen layering along the left chest wall. No
other significant interval change.

B. B. OMDAHL, M.D.

I personally viewed this imaging study and agree with the interpretation
of B. B. OMDAHL, M.D.
BBO/trm   R. L. HAJDIK, M.D.
DD: 07/29/98   DT: 07/29/98

REVIEWING DR.
INITIALS:

ORDER #: 41,42.   CASE#: 3400772236   INVOICE#: 268458,268463
ICD-9: V72.5   FAC CD: IS   MNEM: RAD

SHIELDING: PREGNANT: TECH: No.FILMS:

Page 6:

This report is an analysis from the Nephrologist concerning the right lobe of my liver. They have done a CT Scan and an ultrasound and found a five centimeter (5 cm) mass on my liver while using Sulfur Colloid and tagged RBC cell study. They were also concerned with this being cancerous. This was found on July 29, 1998. I signed myself out of the hospital in August 1998 believing God for miracles concerning my situations.

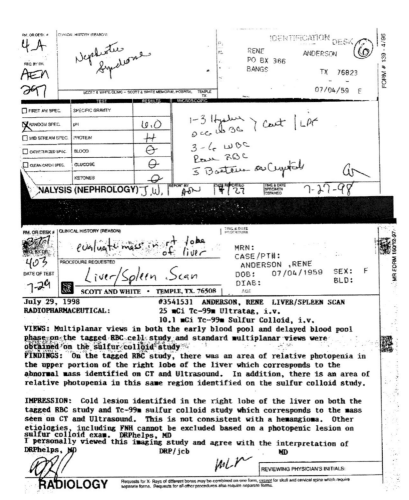

RM. OR DESK #	CLINICAL HISTORY (REASON)				IDENTIFICATION DESK
4-A	Nephrotic Syndrome				RENE ANDERSON
REQ. BY DR.					PO BX 366
AEM					BANGS TX 76823
297					07/04/59 F

SCOTT & WHITE CLINIC – SCOTT & WHITE MEMORIAL HOSPITAL TEMPLE TX

FORM # 139 - 4/96

	TEST	RESULTS	MICROSCOPIC
☐ FIRST AM SPEC.	SPECIFIC GRAVITY		
☒ RANDOM SPEC.	pH	6.0	1-3 Hyalin Cast / LPF
☐ MID STREAM SPEC.	PROTEIN	++	0 cc WBC
☐ CATHETERIZED SPEC.	BLOOD	⊖	3-4 WBC
☐ CLEAN CATCH SPEC.	GLUCOSE	⊖	Rare RBC
	KETONES	⊖	5 Bacteria or Crystals

ANALYSIS (NEPHROLOGY) J.W.   REPORT BY A-N   DATE REPORTED 4/27   TIME & DATE SPECIMEN OBTAINED 7-27-98

RM. OR DESK #	CLINICAL HISTORY (REASON)		TIME & DATE PROCEDURE
	evaluate mass in rt lobe of liver		
REQ. BY DR.			MRN:
403			CASE/PTH:
DATE OF TEST	PROCEDURE REQUESTED		ANDERSON , RENE
7-29	Liver/Spleen Scan		DOB: 07/04/1959 SEX: F
	SCOTT AND WHITE • TEMPLE, TX. 76508		DIAB: BLD:

MR FORM 16012-97

July 29, 1998   #3541531 ANDERSON, RENE LIVER/SPLEEN SCAN
RADIOPHARMACEUTICAL.:   25 mCi Tc-99m Ultratag, i.v.
                          10.1 mCi Tc-99m Sulfur Colloid, i.v.
VIEWS: Multiplanar views in both the early blood pool and delayed blood pool
phase on the tagged RBC cell study and standard multiplanar views were
obtained on the sulfur colloid study
FINDINGS: On the tagged RBC study, there was an area of relative photopenia in
the upper portion of the right lobe of the liver which corresponds to the
abnormal mass identified on CT and Ultrasound. In addition, there is an area of
relative photopenia in this same region identified on the sulfur colloid study.

IMPRESSION: Cold lesion identified in the right lobe of the liver on both the
tagged RBC study and Tc-99m sulfur colloid study which corresponds to the mass
seen on CT and Ultrasound. This is not consistent with a hemangioma. Other
etiologies, including FNH cannot be excluded based on a photopenic lesion on
sulfur colloid exam. DRPhelps, MD
I personally viewed this imaging study and agree with the interpretation of
DRPhelps, MD   DRP/jcb   MD

RADIOLOGY   REVIEWING PHYSICIAN'S INITIALS:

Requests for X- Rays of different bones may be combined on one form, except for skull and cervical spine which require
separate forms. Requests for all other procedures also require separate forms.

Page 7-8:

This is a consult request from the VA Clinic. They are still following me after I left Scott and White and refused to be hospitalized. They see the mass and need to determine if the mass is cancerous. They also request a red-cell liver scan to be done and get an approval for it to be done at the Brownwood Hospital. The order was placed and approved on 12/31/02. Records were received from Scott and White (Page 8) showing that the mass was five centimeters (5 cm), while the VA has it being three centimeters (3cm). So on 01/07/03, the consultation is cancelled because it has shrunk and therefore is benign. Later on, another Dr. does a CT Scan and Ultrasound and cannot find it at all. God does perform miracles if we believe and holdfast to our confession of faith.

Provisional Diagnosis: 3cm liver lesion
Reason For Request:
REASON FOR REQUEST:

43 y/o female has a CT-identified 3cm liver lesion. Differentiation
between malignancy vs hemangioma is needed.

Please schedule for a tagged red cell liver scan, which is done outside
the VA per my understanding.

First hospital requested is Brownwood Regional Hospital, Brownwood,
Texas, at 915-649-3320, or otherwise at Scott & White hospital.

Thank you.

_____APPOINTMENT MADE TO THE FOLLOWING CLINIC (include Date and
Time).

___X__THE CONSULTED SERVICE WILL MAKE APPOINTMENT.

_____NO APPOINTMENT IS NECESSARY FOR THIS CONSULT.

Inter-facility Information
This is not an inter-facility consult request.

Status: DISCONTINUED
Last Action: PRINTED TO

Facility
Activity   Date/Time/Zone   Responsible Person Entered By

CPRS RELEASED ORDER   12/31/02 14:40   CHILDERS,CHARLES   CHILDERS,CHARLES
PRINTED TO B162/A109 12/31/02 14:41
RECEIVED   01/02/03 08:15   ALLING,PANSY   ALLING,PANSY
ADDED COMMENT   01/02/03 09:05   ALLING,PANSY
received for review 12/31/02. approved for fee base for tagged Red Cell
Scan for Liver lesion differentiation between Malignancy vs
hemangioma..to be done at Brownwood Regional or S/W.. Please schedule and
inform Patient of appt.. Thank You

ADDED COMMENT   01/07/03 16:44   CHILDERS,CHARLES   CHILDERS,CHARLES
Records received from Scott & White, showing 5cm hemangioma of the liver,
same as this lesion. Test dated 07/27/1998. This consult is cancelled.
Lesion already evaluated, and benign.

DISCONTINUED   01/07/03 16:44   CHILDERS,CHARLES   CHILDERS,CHARLES
PRINTED TO B162/A109 01/07/03 16:45

PATIENT NAME AND ADDRESS (Mechanical imprinting, if available) | **VISTA Electronic Medical Documentation**

HOOD, RENE
PO BOX 593
Bangs, TEXAS 76823

Printed at CENTRAL TEXAS HCS

Scott & White Radiology

⑧

Name: RENE ANDERSON   Ord. Dr.:   M.D.
MRN#:   Desk/Room: 3STC
DOB: 07/04/1959   Age: Sex: F
Address:
City: State: Zip:

Procedure Requested: ABDOMENCTSCANWWO CONT/PELVISCTSCANWCONTRAST

Date of Study: 07/27/98   Time of Study:
Reason/History: ROABDMASS

ANDERSON, 3
CT SCAN OF THE ABDOMEN AND PELVIS, 07/27/98:
TECHNIQUE: Routine CT scan of the abdomen and pelvis was performed
following uneventful administration of oral and I.V. contrast. Pre-
contrast images as well as delayed images through the liver were also
obtained. No prior CT scans available for comparison.
ABDOMEN:
There are bilateral pleural effusions left greater than right with
associated atelectasis at the lung bases bilaterally. There is a large
amount of free intraperitoneal fluid as well as fluid in the
retroperitoneal spaces. There is a 4.5 x 3.5 cm lesion in the lateral
aspect of the right lobe of the liver. This lesion is hypodense on the
pre-contrasted images and hyperdense on the contrasted images (best seen
on the liver window images). The kidneys are mildly enlarged
bilaterally but otherwise have a normal CT appearance. The spleen,
pancreas, adrenals, gallbladder, and opacified loops of bowel have
normal CT appearance. There are multiple loops of unopacified small
bowel noted throughout the abdomen and pelvis. There is some thickening
of the walls of the stomach however the stomach is non-distended. No
definite intra-abdominal mass, abscess, or adenopathy is identified. A
retro-aortic left renal vein is noted.
PELVIS:
Again noted are multiple loops of unopacified small bowel. There is a
large amount of free fluid in the pelvis. Ovarian cysts are noted
bilaterally. The pelvic organs are otherwise grossly normal. No mass,
abscess, or lymphadenopathy is identified.

IMPRESSION:
1. Bilateral pleural effusions left greater than right with associated
atelectasis.
2. Large amount of free intraperitoneal fluid in the abdomen and pelvis
as well as fluid in the retroperitoneal spaces bilaterally.
3. Ill-defined 4.5 x 3.5 cm lesion in the right lobe of the liver.
This lesion is hypodense on pre-contrasted images and hyperdense on
post-contrasted images. Differential diagnosis includes hemangioma

MR FORM 160 8/97

Pages 9-11:

I am sharing these pages with focus on my voice. My voice had gotten to a place where I could not even generate a whisper from it. My son would have to answer the phone, and I would have to write down my words. You can see on the consult request that my vocal cords had nodules on both sides and they would not close. The specialist said that surgery could help, but he thought that I would never have my voice back. I was also told that the nodules would always remain on my vocal cords. As I smile and think on the goodness of God, I can testify and tell you that they are gone. My vocal cords have been doing great for years and I am able to travel and share the good news! Page 11 is also a short un-descriptive narrative of the battles I was confronted with. Have hope—God will bring you through if you stand (or fall if need be) on the word of God even when the odds are against you. Take it one moment at a time!

DATE OF NOTE: MAR 11, 2002@09:57:26 ENTRY DATE: MAR 11, 2002@09:57:26
    AUTHOR: SETZER,LINDA C   EXP COSIGNER:
    URGENCY: STATUS: COMPLETED

PER CONSULT REQUEST: MAILED RIGHT AND LEFT MEDIUM WRIST SPLINTS BY
CERTIFIED MAIL TO VET'S ADDRESS AND DOCUMENTED 2319 WITH ISSUES

/es/ LINDA C SETZER
PURCHASING AGENT
Signed: 03/11/2002 09:58
==
=============================== END ================================

Current PC Provider: CHILDERS,CHARLES S
Current Pat. Status: Outpatient
Primary Eligibility: SC LESS THAN 50%

Order Information
To Service: T SLP VOICE
Attention: VENUS,CAROL A
From Service: ZT ENT NEW PATIENT NEW
Requesting Provider: ALVERSON,EDWARD D
Service is to be rendered on an OUTPATIENT basis
Place: Consultant's choice
Urgency: Routine
Orderable Item: T SLP VOICE
Consult: Consult Request
Provisional Diagnosis: Vocal cord nodules with hoarseness
Reason For Request:
  42yo, -   black female known to you with vocal cord nodules and
  hoarseness in the past wishes re-evaluation.
_____APPOINTMENT MADE TO THE FOLLOWING CLINIC (Include Date and Time).

_____APPOINTMENT WILL BE MADE BY THE CONSULTING SERVICE.

_____NO APPOINTMENT IS NECESSARY FOR THIS CONSULT.

Inter-facility Information
This is not an inter-facility consult request.

Status: SCHEDULED
Last Action: SCHEDULED

Facility
Activity   Date/Time/Zone   Responsible Person Entered By

PATIENT NAME AND ADDRESS (Mechanical imprinting, if available) | **VISTA Electronic Medical Documentation**

HOOD, RENE
PO BOX 593
Bangs, TEXAS 76823   Printed at CENTRAL TEXAS HCS

```
Facility
  Activity              Date/Time/Zone     Responsible Person  Entered By
-------------------------------------------------------------------------------
  CPRS RELEASED ORDER   01/11/02 16:26     MARKENA,RAMA        ABEITA,LUPITA S
  PRINTED TO            01/11/02 16:26                         ABEITA,LUPITA S
    ENT$PRT (BIG)
  SCHEDULED             01/14/02 09:30     STEWART,ANNE        STEWART,ANNE
2/27@930

  INCOMPLETE RPT        02/28/02 15:09     ALVERSON,EDWARD D   DAVENPORT,CARL S
    Note# 7401548
  COMPLETE/UPDATE       03/04/02 08:47     ALVERSON,EDWARD D   RANEY,LEWIS A
    Note# 7401548

Note: TIME ZONE is local if not indicated
-------------------------------------------------------------------------------

    TITLE: ENT CONSULT RESULTS
DATE OF NOTE: FEB 27, 2002@13:29       ENTRY DATE: FEB 28, 2002@15:08:37
    AUTHOR: ALVERSON,EDWARD D       EXP COSIGNER: RANEY,LEWIS A
    URGENCY:                             STATUS: COMPLETED

HOOD, RENE G
```

ENT CONSULTATION

SUBJECTIVE: This 42-year-old  black female presents to the ENT clinic with complaint of pain and swelling on the right side of the neck, which is intermittent in nature. The patient has noted this problem for approximately the past year and although she has had problems on both sides of her neck, it has been predominantly on the right side. She describes this as swelling underneath her jaw in the area of the angle of the jaw down into the neck, which becomes larger and more tender until she is treated with antibiotic therapy, at which time it seems to reduce in size. She has been concerned about the use of antibiotic therapy over and over and in recent times as avoided use of antibiotic therapy with spontaneous remission in these swellings.

Today, she presents complaining of mainly tenderness down in the throat. This patient has a history of vocal cord nodules with subsequent hoarseness. However, she has been seen previously in this clinic and states today that her hoarseness is actually better than it was in years

---

PATIENT NAME AND ADDRESS (Mechanical imprinting, if available) | **VISTA Electronic Medical Documentation**

HOOD, RENE
PO BOX 593
Bangs, TEXAS 76823

Printed at CENTRAL TEXAS HCS

RHEUMATOLOGY CONSULTATION

DATE OF BIRTH: 4 JULY 1959

DATE OF CONSULTATION: 25 OCT 01

HISTORY/PRESENT ILLNESS: Consultation regarding history of lupus .
Computerized notes are the only notes available. All of those
were reviewed. The patient does have some medical records from private
setting at home. She was advised to bring for a review next visit.

This is a 42-year-old African-American woman with the following medical
history:

1.   History of possible lupus. Admitted to Scott & White Hospital in
August 1998 with evidence of fluid retention and proteinuria. Had renal
biopsy done after the biopsy, was recommended to have chemotherapy. Sounds
 The patient left the hospital against
medical advice.

2.   Chronic anemia with leukopenia, also has evidence of iron
deficiency. Seen Hematology Dec. 2000. Note was reviewed, conclusion was
anemia, leukopenia, and recurrent sinus infections. The patient was
discharged from the clinic to be followed by a primary M.D. with
recommendations on the laboratory reports.

3.   History of chronic hoarseness of voice. Had seen ENT in private
as well as at the VA. The VA visit was May 1999 - conclusion was
bilateral vocal nodules. Had indirect laryngoscopy done. Recommendation
was to have a speech therapy consult, which she received.

4.   History of abnormal mammogram with calcifications, with
micro-calcifications. She saw Surgery, had biopsy done Jan. 2001, report
has evidence of marked fibrocystic disease. Negative for malignancy.

5.   History of recurrent urinary tract infection as well as sinus
infections last 3-4 years.

6.   History of allergies, seen allergist on fee base in May 2000.
Conclusion was chronic perennial rhinitis, both allergic and vascular
type. Allergic conjunctivitis, mild contact dermatitis. Recommendation
was environmental control and use of antihistamines.
PAST MEDICAL HISTORY:

PAST SURGICAL HISTORY: Removal of ectopic pregnancy and had renal biopsy
done in 1998.

PATIENT NAME AND ADDRESS (Mechanical imprinting, if available)

VISTA Electronic Medical Documentation

HOOD, RENE
PO BOX 593
Bangs, TEXAS 76823

Printed at CENTRAL TEXAS HCS

Pages 12-19

These pages detail, in part, the four months after I signed myself out of the hospital. The Dr. will state that I was depressed in his general assessment, but I truly was not. I was more agitated with him trying to get me to become compliant with methods I felt would harm me and cause dependency. You will read his many attempts to persuade me otherwise and also his amazement with my test results after not complying with his recommendations.

Look at how within 4 months my kidney began to function properly with hope and the word and power of God. I am so grateful that our Savior lives! Please read and rejoice with me as you see and comprehend the willingness and almightiness of God to do all that He said He would do. I believe and know that God is not a respect of a person. He will do it for you! Hope, expect, and release your faith, He will give you the miracle that you need.

HISTORY OF PRESENT ILLNESS: She is seen today for follow up of her lupus, proteinuria, ascites and angioedema/? photosensitivity. I spoke briefly with Dr. Folkes who cared for her along with Dr. Nichol at Scott and White and she apparently had fairly extensive evaluation. Her renal biopsy had to be done open and this was suggestive of a type of peripheral nephropathy. She was started on Prednisone 20 t.i.d. and recommendations were that she would probably need Cyclophosphamide however in the course of her evaluation she was also noted to have an exudate of ascites and there was a mass in her liver. They recommended needle biopsy of this liver lesion prior to doing the Cyclophosphamide but Ms. Anderson was apparently not willing to do this and refused it and wanted to go home. She obviously was explained the risks of this. Since going home four or five days ago, she actually is doing relatively well. She has some mild discomfort at her incision site that seems expected. She feels like her swelling of her abdomen in down some. She has had some peripheral edema though none at this time. Her facial swelling is variable but not bad today.

CURRENT MEDICATIONS: At present include she is on the Prednisone 20 t.i.d. She doesn't take anything else at this time. She was also restarted on iron therapy.

ALLERGIES: None.

REVIEW OF SYSTEMS: She denies any headaches. No new neurologic symptoms. No shortness of breath. No chest pain. No bloody stools or black stools.

PHYSICAL EXAMINATION:

GENERAL: Alert and oriented, depressed appearing.

VITAL SIGNS: Blood pressure is 140/82. Weight is down to 162.

HEENT: She has some minimal facial swelling. Oropharynx is clear.

ABDOMEN: There is some mild diffuse tenderness mostly at the incision site but no erythema and her wound appears to be healing very well.

EXTREMITIES: No edema at this time.

NEUROLOGIC: Unchanged.

IMPRESSION AND PLAN:

1. LUPUS

2. EXUDATE OF ASCITES

3. DEPRESSION

4. PROTEINURIA

5. LUPUS NEPHROPATHY

6. IRON DEFICIENCY ANEMIA

7. PREVIOUS LEUKOPENIA

8/10/98 Continued.................

8. HEPATIC MASS

I spoke at length to Ms. Anderson regarding all her problems, the prognosis with and without treatment and the risks of not undergoing treatment or further evaluation of these problems. I think she obviously needs to be evaluated further, both to see what this hepatic mass is and so she can be treated appropriately for her nephropathy. She is adamantly opposed to doing anything at this time. I am simply going to follow her for now and see her back in two weeks and we will rediscuss these problems. If she has any acute worsening, she knows to call me. When I see her back, I am going to check a chemistry, a CBC and check a dip of her urine. I am also going to do a quick sonogram and see how much ascites she has at this time but she seems obviously be having some resolution. I am going to put her back on Lasix at just 40 a day and we will watch her weight. If she has any further problems, she knows to call me.

SO:jm

Dictated: 8/10/98
Typed: 8/11/98

cc:

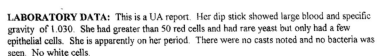

Anderson, Rene

8/24/98

LABORATORY DATA: This is a UA report. Her dip stick showed large blood and specific gravity of 1.030. She had greater than 50 red cells and had rare yeast but only had a few epithelial cells. She is apparently on her period. There were no casts noted and no bacteria was seen. No white cells.

SO:jm

Dictated: 8/24/98
Typed: 8/25/98

8/25/98

HISTORY OF PRESENT ILLNESS: She is seen today for follow up of her lupus nephritis, anemia and possible hepatic mass. In general she is doing better. Her fluid is down significantly. She denies any pains. No shortness of breath. She has been prescribed Prednisone 20 mg. t.i.d. although she is certainly not taking this. At best, she has been taking 20 a day. We had another very long discussion about her various problems, her prognosis especially about treatment and she seems to understand the importance of this at times and at other times she seems'to be in complete denial. ─ no denial, just faith!
REVIEW OF SYSTEMS: She denies any headache. No neurologic symptoms. No abdominal pain, urinary symptoms or changes in stools.
CURRENT MEDICATIONS: Listed on her previous notes.
SONOGRAM: Her abdominal sonogram showed just a minimal amount of ascites and that is obviously dramatically improved.
PHYSICAL EXAMINATION:
GENERAL: She is alert and oriented in no distress.
VITAL SIGNS: Her blood pressure is normal.
HEENT: Normocephalic. Atraumatic. Pupils are reactive. Extraocular muscles are intact. Oropharynx is clear.
NECK: Supple.
CHEST: Clear to auscultation.
HEART: Regular.
ABDOMEN: Soft and nontender. Good bowel sounds. .
EXTREMITIES: No edema.

IMPRESSION AND PLAN: I am going to back off her Lasix to once a day and check a urine and some lab work and again we spoke at length. She is somewhat opposed to going back to Temple to have the biopsy done. I am going to see if we can have radiation do a CT guided biopsy here. I informed her she needs to take her Prednisone three times a day and she said she will start doing this. As soon as we get a diagnosis on this liver lesion, we will consider

8/25/98 Continued........................

Cyclophosphamide treatment too and we will get her back to nephrology for that. She is somewhat opposed to this at this time but we will continue to discuss it with her.

SO:jm

Dictated: 8/26/98
Typed: 8/27/98

cc:

9/4/98

HISTORY OF PRESENT ILLNESS: She is seen as a work in with some sore throat and fever. She has also had a little bit of mild shortness of breath and some palpitations this morning. She had her lab done this week including a basic chemistry which showed normal renal functions and a potassium of 3.1. She had been diuresed down significantly and hasn't been on Potassium. Her urine protein impressively in 24 hours was only 183 which is down from several hundred. Her urine showed a few white cells but many epithelial cells and no red cells were noted. She is taking her Prednisone intermittently and we talked at length again about the need for her to be compliant with her care. She has had some low grade temperatures since last night and this morning she feels generally just a little bit "achy" with some general myalgias but no joint swelling, no erythema. No chest pains. She felt just a little bit of palpitations this morning. No lightheadedness or dizziness. No abdominal pains. Her wound is healing nicely with no problems there.

REVIEW OF SYSTEMS: Otherwise essentially unremarkable.

PAST MEDICAL HISTORY: Well documented on previous notes.

PHYSICAL EXAMINATION:

VITAL SIGNS: Blood pressure today is 132/84. Weight is down to 145. Temperature is 100.6 and pulse is 108.

HEENT: Normocephalic. Atraumatic. Pupils are reactive. Extraocular muscles are intact. Oropharynx - she has some mild pharyngeal erythema.

NECK: Supple. No lymphadenopathy.

CHEST: Clear to auscultation.

HEART: Regular. No S3. No S4.

ABDOMEN: Soft and nontender. Good bowel sounds. Her wound is essentially almost healed.

EXTREMITIES: No edema.

IMPRESSION AND PLAN: 1. LUPUS

2. LUPUS NEPHRITIS

3. HEPATIC MASS

4. UPPER RESPIRATORY INFECTION

5. FEVER

I expect her fever is due to infection although she obviously concerns me especially with her noncompliant use of her medications. She is instructed again that she needs to take her Prednisone as instructed and I put her on Trovan 200 a day for seven days. She has stopped her Lasix and her fluid status appears normal to possibly mildly hypovolemic. I am going to give her K-Dur to replace her Potassium and I will recheck that again on follow up. Her hepatic mass was reevaluated using interval scanning of the CT and it did not have the pattern of the malignant lesion but rather suggestive of a cavernous meningioma and it was recommended to follow this up in three months. It was felt that biopsy was not indicated at this time. I will get her to see nephrology again. She is deciding if she wants to go back to Scott and White. She had some problem with that, I think more related to her anxieties with everything that was going on at the time but she is to let me know when she decides what she wants to do. I have given recommendations that we continue Prednisone at the current dose and get her seen by nephrology and possibly start Cyclophosphamide but she doesn't want to do this at this time. She is in fact improved with regard to her kidney function although I am still very concerned. She is planning on going out of town this weekend. I told her if she is not significantly improved by tomorrow morning that she is not to go out of town that if she worsens, she is to call me immediately.

SO:jm

ADDENDUM: Because of her palpitations, I am going to go ahead and check an EKG and make sure there is no conduction disturbance and also she has had some mild shortness of breath this morning, I am going to repeat her chest x-ray although she really sounds quite good on exam.

SO:jm

Dictated: 9/4/98
Typed: 9/6/98

HISTORY OF PRESENT ILLNESS: She is seen for follow up of her lupus. She continues to be somewhat noncompliant with her medications. She is however taking 40 a day of the Prednisone. She is supposed to be taking 60 a day. Also we had talked about wanting to put her on Cyclophosphamide. She refuses to do this. I explained that this may in fact lead to renal failure and potentially death. She feel fully willing to take those risks, feeling confident that God want let her be hurt by this. She has had some mild sore throat since I last saw her. She describes some facial rash and actually some discolored lesions on her arms and face also. She has continued photosensitivity although this is mild at this time. She denies any shortness of breath. No chest pain. No abdominal pain or urinary symptoms.

PHYSICAL EXAMINATION:

GENERAL: She is alert and oriented in no distress.

HEENT: She has some erythematous ___ /m /m ___ rash that is not totally confluent although there are areas of confluence. Her oropharynx is clear except for some minimal pharyngeal erythema.

NECK: Supple. No adenopathy.

CHEST: Clear.

HEART: Regular. No S3. No S4.

ABDOMEN: Soft and nontender. Good bowel sounds. Wound is completely healed.

IMPRESSION AND PLAN: 1. SYSTEMIC LUPUS ERYTHEMATOSUS

                                 2. LUPUS NEPHRITIS

                                 3. DERMATITIS, SECONDARY TO LUPUS

We talked about options. I told her at least I would increase her steroid and I felt like she needed to be on Cytoxan given her renal involvement. She is opposed to this. She said she would consider it if her protein levels are still elevated in her urine. I explained that she needed to see a nephrologist regardless but she is opposed to it at this time. She understands the risks obviously. I am going to check a repeat UA and see if she has any protein there. As always if she has any problems, she knows to call. I am going to continue to follow her closely. I will see her back in a couple of weeks and we will call her with her UA results.

SO:jm

Dictated: 9/18/98
Typed: 9/20/98

* The protein levels did drop.

HISTORY OF PRESENT ILLNESS: She is seen today for follow up of her lupus nephritis and anemia. She is only taking her Prednisone 20 or 40 a day. She denies any symptoms. She really feels much better. She is having no fatigue. No skin symptoms.
CURRENT MEDICATIONS: At this time just the Prednisone and some p.r.n. Zyrtec.
REVIEW OF SYSTEMS: No headaches. No neurologic complaints. No abdominal pain or urinary symptoms. No changes in stools.
PHYSICAL EXAMINATION:
GENERAL: Alert and oriented. Really looks quite healthy today.
SKIN: Her skin is clear. No angioedema or rashes.
HEENT: Oropharynx is clear.
NECK: Supple.
CHEST: Clear to auscultation.
HEART: Regular. No S3. No S4.
ABDOMEN: Soft and nontender. Good bowel sounds.
EXTREMITIES: No edema.

IMPRESSION AND PLAN: 1. LUPUS

2. LUPUS NEPHRITIS

3. ANEMIA

Her lab previously showed sed rate of 24, creatinine was .6 and interestingly her sodium was 127. I am going to recheck that today. Her most recent lab had shown some significant anemia. I also want to recheck a blood count today. If she has any further problems, she is to call me. I am going to get her set up to see Dr. Cox in Abilene regarding possible Cytoxan treatment.

SO:jm

Dictated: 10/02/98
Typed: 10/04/98

HISTORY OF PRESENT ILLNESS: She is seen today for follow up of her lupus, lupus nephritis, dermatitis. In general she is doing quite well. She has some occasional irregularity of her periods but no significant heavy flow with her most recent period. She saw Dr. Cox up in Abilene who is still awaiting some of her records from Scott and White before making final recommendations. She has had no problems urinating. No problems with swelling in her feet. No urinary symptoms. No shortness of breath. No chest pain. No abdominal pain. She has had some problems with some occasional swelling of her face which she has had in the past. It looks good today. She has some occasional what sounds like folliculitis around her mouth. She really describes more perioral dermatitis and mass related to her steroids.

PAST MEDICAL HISTORY: Well documented on previous notes.

CURRENT MEDICATIONS: Prednisone 20 a day and p.r.n. Zyrtec.

REVIEW OF SYSTEMS: No headaches. No visual complaints. No urinary symptoms or changes in her stools.

PHYSICAL EXAMINATION:

GENERAL: She is alert and oriented in no distress. Generally health appearing young female.

HEENT: Normocephalic. Atraumatic. No angioedema or dermatitis noted except for just a few small areas of folliculitis around on her chin.

NECK: Supple.

CHEST: Clear to auscultation.

HEART: Regular. No S3.

ABDOMEN: Benign.

EXTREMITIES: No edema.

IMPRESSION AND PLAN: 1. LUPUS, LUPUS NEPHRITIS

                            2. PERIORAL DERMATITIS

I put her on some Doxycycline twice a day for the next ten days. We will consider further treatment if she has recurrence of that. Continue her Prednisone at the present and she is to follow up with Dr. Cox. I will see her back in a couple of months.

SO:jm

Dictated: 12/02/98
Typed: 12/03/98

Pages 20-21

These last two pages represent what's currently happening in my life with lab and circumstances. Again, enjoy reading it and then join with me in a shout of victory! I am so thankful to God. This was not an easy journey, and I do not think that life's journeys are very easy. We stumble, fall, get bruised and cut, but if we are determined to have the last word as Christ did, we are going to have to participate in the battle and say as He did, "It is written." That is all I did—trust and have faith in the word of God, and it proved itself trustworthy. Have faith in God and all that He has said.

Sima Pandey, MD
582 Concord Road, Suite A
Smyrna, GA 30082

Phone: 404-417-1760
Fax: 404-417-1770

December 6, 2010

Rene Hood

Dear Ms. Hood:

I am writing to give you results from your tests on 12/03/2010.

Your total cholesterol was 189, which is normal. Your HDL cholesterol, which is the good type, was 70, which is in the good range. Your LDL cholesterol, which is the type associated with heart disease, was 107. The LDL should be below 130 for most patients, and below 100 for patients with diabetes or heart disease. Your triglycerides, which is the measure of fat in the blood, was 61, which is in the good range. Your cholesterol levels are normal. No treatment for cholesterol is needed at this time.

Your blood sugar, which checks for diabetes, was 77, which is in the normal range. Normal is below 110. There is no evidence for diabetes.

The liver enzymes were normal.

Your renal function was normal.

If you see other physicians that may be interested in your results, the numbers for some of the key labs are: Hgb 10.9, Hct 35.2, Plts 94, Na 138, K 3.6, Ca 9.0, Cr 0.9, BUN 11, ALT 21, AST 35, T.Bili 0.7.

The following tests were all normal: Renal Function, Liver Enzymes, Potassium, Calcium, Sodium, White Blood Cells.

Your blood count was low on your lab tests which means that you are anemic. When you receive this letter, please return to the clinic on Tuesday, Wednesday, or Thursday between 7:30 and 9:00 am for additional bloodwork to look for the cause of your anemia. You do not need to be fasting and do not need an appointment. Also, I am having the nurse send you some stool cards to look for blood in your stool. You can have blood in your stool and not see it. Please complete the cards and mail them back to the VAMC as instructed on the packet as soon as possible.

Your future appointments are as follows:
    12/23/2010 14:00   SMR PC-WOMENS WELLNESS

Sincerely,

Sima Pandey, MD

Sima Pandey, MD
2041 Mesa Valley Way, Ste 185
Austell, GA 30106

Phone: 404-329-2222
Fax: 404-417-1770

July 14, 2011

Rene Hood

Dear Ms. Hood:

I am writing to give you results from your tests on 07/13/2011.

Your thyroid test was normal.

If you see other physicians that may be interested in your results, the numbers for some of the key labs are: Hgb 11.8, Hct 37.2, Plts 134, TSH 0.73.

The following tests were all normal: Thyroid, Anemia.

Sincerely,

Sima Pandey, MD

Appendix B

Philosophy Thesis

<u>**I propose that no individual can have quality of life and fulfill their dreams or goals without hope.**</u> I will attempt to prove this by first defining hope and what I mean by <u>"quality of life."</u> I will attempt to show, though hope isn't seen, nor can one hold hope within the palm of one's hand that hope is as tangible as a piece of fruit of which we partake each day. I will further attempt to show <u>the nature of hope</u> and how it provides energy to our mind, body, and spirit. I will attempt to do this by comparing philosophical theories, by the understanding of what philosophy is, by personal experiences of others and myself, and any other material I may come upon as I search out this matter.

I will start by giving the definition of hope according to the Standard Encyclopedic Dictionary. It states that hope is: 1. To desire with expectation of fulfillment. 2. To wish; want. 3. To have desire or expectation, (to hope against hope).

Let us first analyze this definition. To desire means: to long for something, to crave or to seek after a thing with a great passion. The second part of the definition says with expectation. What does this mean? I believe "with expectation" means to anticipate. But what are we anticipating but the last part of the definition which states "of fulfillment". I believe we will agree that fulfillment means to bring about the accomplishment of something. Now that we have the definition of hope let us look into the true nature of it. What is hope, within itself? How do we explain its nature or character?

I will begin by saying, when we wish to have something this isn't the same as hope. Individuals may wish for all kinds of things that they know there is no chance of them obtaining. Therefore, in order for one to have hope, one must speculate that there is a possibility of achievement. For me to truly contemplate something I must have expectation of fulfilling that which I have contemplated. If I tried to contemplate something, where there is no expectation of it being fulfilled, it cannot be accomplished. I can wish for something but I cannot contemplate such a thing. I can wish to explore the sea by swimming for seven days straight without coming up for air, but I cannot hope to accomplish this, therefore I cannot contemplate to do so,

I conclude from this that the definition of hope is to have a craving to seek after a thing with great passion with anticipation that it will be accomplished. I propose within this definition we find structure and comfort. Why do I use the words structure and comfort? I use them anticipating that from this definition one can begin to see that hope, though it be a four letter word, provides mankind with a combination of relating parts. I present that hope is a pathway that has been paved upon stable and proven grounds through the centuries. One begins this journey with one's desire of any one thing, it doesn't matter if the thing is said to be big or small. The object of one's desire isn't important as how one's desire will be completed. I also said that the four letter word hope provided mankind with comfort I believe that all will agree that comfort is a state of either mental or physical ease. I propose to you that the ease or comfort that one received is in relationship with the structure that is presented by hope. The structure being the "nature of hope" expressing the possibilities of accomplishment.

In the wording "Quality of Life", I simply mean fruitful and productive relationships. "Quality of Life" is arriving at a place of accepting that one has strength and weakness, ability and inability, and then using them all for the good of oneself, the good of your family, friends, neighbors, and the good of the world. This is what I propose is "Quality of Life.

I would now like to look at the tangibility of hope and in doing so I would like to look at some of the philosophers that have shared with us their insight on many matters. Let us start with the Greek philosopher Plato and the Myth of the Cave. Plato describes the climb of ignorance as from a dark cave upward and then out into the light of wisdom, knowledge, and understanding. The emotions of this plight would be devastating. The long walk up the corridor one would hear screams from within oneself compelling them to go back, saying, "Do not go out in the light". Negativity would arise from within one's reasoning to discuss safety issues because this light has not yet been experienced so there is no reference to establish boundaries. I venture to say that hope was present in the midst of fear and it was the hope of bettering oneself that persuaded ignorance to continue its climb. The reason I state that hope was present and a tangible force behind ignorance's climb is because without the presence of hope, fear would have taken over and ended the climb. I know that in each one of our lives we can remember when we were on a journey desiring to fulfill a dream. If only as a child, playing a sport and wanting so badly to score the winning point. But fear rises from the thought of what could happen if the shot is missed and though you're right there under the basket and have a clear shot you pass it on to someone you think is a better player. You did not allow hope to give you the drive you needed to take the chance of missing the shot and become the one who made the winning shot. The very nature of hope would have given you a glance of the possibility of that which you intended. Because hope was not present you are pushed back, your gifts and talents are suppressed and your true abilities may never surface.

Socrates made a statement before his accusers that "I tell you that wealth does not make you good within, but that from inner goodness come wealth and every other benefit to man." As I read this I propose that even the great philosopher Socrates proclaims that what I called the "quality of life" is what he describes as inner goodness. I will attempt to take this a little further by saying that the inner goodness which is within man, lives in a dark place and can only see shades and figures of what is called truth. The longing for goodness is to see and understand so that it might excel and share all of the wealth that is enclosed within it. The key factor is hope. Hope reexamines the circumstances and acknowledges what is reality or true. Then hope revisits the desire for validation. After validation is established, hope reviews the desire and offers strength and assurance for the journey. Let's understand something here; hope does not claim that the journey will be a simple one but the opposite.

I would chance to say that mostly all things that can be attained in life have value. I have learned through reading and words of my philosophy teacher, Mr. B. that "the value of philosophy is that through it we achieve freedom; freedom from assumptions we have unquestioningly accepted from others, and freedom to decide for ourselves what we believe about ourselves and our place in the universe". I will step out and argue that hope also offers freedom to each one of us. When we walk in fear we are constantly looking over our shoulders or to the left and the right. This means that our focus isn't on what is before us. In our hastiness we could overlook so many things that would be profitable to us.

As my counter-argument I would propose that hope is just a sensation of the mind and that it holds no actuality in the world of reality. I will assume the argument of determinism and say that human actions are determine, I will argue that this four lettered word that supposedly contains great strength and endurance is simply a phase in life that one goes through from time to time. Life in general for each individual has been perfectly determined before their birth and no matter what one does within their lifespan the end results will still be that which was determined for you before your birth. Through the century's cases have been represented to the courts for actions of murder, whether crimes of passion or not, the charges were withdrawn because it was established that the individual had only fulfilled what was determined of him.

This prime objective which is determined, to carry out your purpose in life is interwoven within your character, gifts, and talents. If hoped or had a desire it would be from that which has already been predetermined for your life. One will not have a desire to be the individual to score the winning point if it is not predetermined for him/her to make the winning score. I argue that if the ball is passed to another and he/she scores it is because of the predetermined destiny of his/her life.

Hope is not real, nor is it tangible. It holds no greatness or worth. It will not assist anyone throughout theirs journey in life. As for the Myth of the Cave, knowledge will be revealed at the time and place that it has been predetermined to be released. It will enlighten the individual who has been predetermined to receive the revelation of its knowledge.

In conclusion I would state that nothing happens by chance or accidentally. If you are a poor person and you hope to be rich one day, stop hoping because hope is just a game that we play. The person that has been predetermined to be rich will be the one who inherits richness, whether he or she is conscious of their destiny or not.

I proposed that the counter-argument has no validity. No proof was given to substantiate these statements opposing hope. Nor were any statistics or facts given to validate the predetermined destiny of an individual.

Therefore, I conclude that **hope** is essential! No individual can have a "quality of life" and fulfill their dreams or goals in life without hope. In order for the Wright brothers to achieve flight so many years ago, they had to first have a dream? Can you for a moment, image them laying on their backs and looking up at the sky and then seeing one bird after another fly over their heads? In amazement, they are challenged with the thought that man can also fly given the right equipment. Let's move forward in time until we come to 1961. What do you think empowered Alan B. Shepard? Here you have a man who does not know what to expect. He only knows that he hopes to experience something no one has done before. In other words, he contemplates that it is possible to travel to outer space.

In the Bible in the book of Romans chapter eight verses 24-25 it says "For we are saved by **hope**; but hope that is seen is not hope: for what a man see, why does he yet hope for? But if we hope for that we see not, then do we with patience wait for it.

I would have to agree with this analysis. Let take a moment to dissect and examine what the Apostle Paul is truly trying to convey to us in this first segment; "For we are saved by hope", I propose that in this statement we could conclude that saved means freed and to attain freedom we must have hope of one day being set free. Without a doubt I know that all of the great African American men and women who sacrificed themselves for freedom had a great hope in their heart. To think that a slave would attempt to run away from a plantation and not have hope within his or her heart of freedom would be senseless. Can you argue that they would run for pleasure? That they would run just to have a change of daily routines? I seriously doubt that any of us would come to that conclusion. These men and women knew that if they did not succeed that they would be brutally punished and even put to death but they ran. Did they run in assurance that the master would understand their position in the matter? Did they run knowing that at any given time someone would rise up and take their defense? I say not! But they ran with a desire of expectation to see those expectations accomplished. They ran with a deep and passionate yearning that they could not describe to even their other family members at times. They ran with a craving to be free, to make choices for themselves and for their family and they ran with hope pumping fuel through their veins saying that there is light at the end of the tunnel. Hope saying, freedom id possible. Did Rosa parks sit at the front of the bus overwhelmed with fear? Did fear encumber her mind, heart, and soul? She was considered lower than the whites on the bus. She was at that instant breaking the law! She was sitting in a seat that was designated for whites only! What was this woman thinking or was she thinking at all? I propose the she had been waiting with patience for the opportunity to make the right move to seal the fruition of her dream. She knew within herself that it was possible for one black woman to make one of the greatest differences in the movement for the advancement of colored people. Why was she able to do this? She had **hope**. Are we seeing here the propelling or even compelling nature of hope?

Again, I conclude that the grace of hope was present saying to her in an assuring manner that this is a step that will break down walls of prejudice and discrimination. That this step, even if it causes you your life will bring a better life to African Americans of future generations.

As the Apostle stated, "hope that is seen is not hope", for what a man (woman) sees why then is there reason for them to hope. Rosa parks did not see in her natural senses Black men and women of all nationalities sitting at the front of the bus, but she saw it as she hoped it to be in hope.

I conclude that each one of us whether we are small, big, tall, short, black, white, Muslim, Catholic, Christian, Jew, male or female need hope to contend with the complexities of this world and the day to day dramas that society reveals. This is by far not a perfect world that we live in but it is all that we have presently.

As I conclude, I challenge us to walk through this life with such passion that no trial or tribulation of any magnitude would relinquish the flames of our desire of living a "quality life" and fulfilling our dreams and goals. **Carry hope with you and slay all your giants!**

References

Excerpt from Frank A. Gerbode, M.D. (2001)

Kings James Study Bible

Standard Encyclopedic Dictionary

Philosophy text book written by Manuel Velasquez

Quotations: from the apostle Paul in the book of Romans, Socrates and Plato

I pray that all of you understood the argument and received the power of the truth and the strength of hope. It has truly been my pleasure and honor to present this thesis and this book to you for the glory of God. Be blessed and walk in the riches of His glory!

Rene' G. Hood

To contact Rene' G. Hood for speaking engagements:

Brenda Green (Personal assistant): <u>rojministries@live.com</u>
(301) 643-7347

or

Root of Jesse Ministry
P.O. Box 1305
Smyrna, GA 30082
<u>www.Rootofjesseministry.com</u>

CPSIA information can be obtained at www.ICGtesting.com
Printed in the USA
BVOW081629230712

295939BV00001BA/1/P